How to Turn Your Screenplay into a Novel

Lindsey Hughes

Copyright © 2024 by Lindsey Hughes and Pitch Master Press

All rights reserved.

No portion of this book may be reproduced in any form without written permission from the publisher or author, except as permitted by U.S. copyright law.

ISBNs:

979-8-9910873-0-8 - paperback

979-8-9910873-1-5 - digital book

979-8-9910873-2-2 - hardback

Contents

Dedication	VII
Introduction	IX

Part One:
Getting Ready to Write

Part One: Getting Ready to Write	1
Step 1: Read in Your Genre	3
Step 2: Read Your Screenplay	10
Step 3: Write a Scene Breakdown	13
Step 4: Build Your Email List	20
Step 5: Build Your Website	31
Step 6: Choose Your POV	36
Step 7: Converting Your Screenplay Into Prose with Scrivener	49

Part Two
Writing Your Novel

Part Two: Writing Your Novel	61
Step 8: Start With the Dialogue	62
Step 9: Add Detail	73
Step 10: Building Your Novel's Structure With Chapters	90

Part Three:
After Writing

Part Three: After Writing	105
Step 11: Hire an Editor	106
Step 12: Hire a Cover Designer	118
Step 13: Write Your Book Blurb	125
Step 14: Write Your Bio	138
Step 15: Get a Headshot	144
Step 16: Write Your Back Matter	146

Step 17: Format Your Book 151
  Why is Book Formatting Important?
  Basic Steps in Book Formatting
  Formatting Tools for Indie Authors
  Take Aways
  Action Steps

Part Four:
Publish Your Book

Part Four: Publish Your Book	159
All About Indie Publishing	160

Step 18: Get an ISBN	165
Step 19: Get Your Copyright	169
Step 20: Upload Your E-book to Retailers	174
Step 21: Upload Your Book to Print on Demand Services	194
Conclusion	212

Checklists & Resources

Checklists & Resources	213
Checklist	214
Author Resources	217
Publishing Budget	223
Take Aways & Action Steps	225

Acknowledgements	251
About the Author	253
Also by	255

For all the writers of untold stories

Introduction

Why turn your screenplay into a book? What is your unsold, unproduced screenplay doing for you besides gathering digital dust on your hard drive? It is your idea, your intellectual property. Why not get your story out into the world and make some money?

How do you do share your story and make a profit? Turn it into a novel and publish it yourself!

Independent publishing has been going strong since the debut of the Kindle in 2007. Gone is the stigma of a self-published book. Millions of authors are making a living publishing their own books.

As self-published authors, they have complete control over their material. They decide when to publish, where to publish, what the cover art will be, and how to promote their book. This experience of being an independently published author is a 180 degree turn away from being a screenwriter.

The life of a screenwriter is waiting for someone to say yes. Yes, we like your writing. Yes, we'll buy your screenplay. Yes, we'll green light your screenplay. This is a long, arduous, and heart-breaking process, whether you are a newbie or a seasoned writer.

And most screenplays never sell, let alone get produced. So why not take your screenplay that you spent your blood, sweat, and tears creating, and turn it into a book? After all, stories are for sharing.

With a novel, you have access to a large and enthusiastic audience. Book readers love stories, and they are always looking for their next favorite book. Turning your screenplay into a novel is the first step to building an audience of superfans that love your stories and look forward to the next one.

It's a win-win situation. Your story sees the light of day and you make money off of it. Once your book is published, if you continue to market it, it will continue to find new readers and earn you money.

Even better, you're not starting from scratch. Your screenplay is an outline for your novel, and you know these characters inside and out. You already have done the hard work of creating a story out of nothing.

The Novel Way of Thinking

When you write a screenplay, you're not just creating a story; you're crafting a blueprint for a film. Because of the constrictions of time and budget in film production, unnecessary details are cut. In contrast, novels give writers creative freedom to explore characters, settings, and storylines in depth. Unlike screenplays, where the length and visual medium limits the scope of storytelling, novels are limitless.

Transforming your screenplay into a novel opens up a vast territory of creative possibilities. You can explore and expand your characters, story, and world, bringing your story to life in ways that a screenplay can't.

In a screenplay, the audience learns everything from dialogue and acting, while in a novel the reader is inside the characters' heads, experiencing firsthand their thoughts and feelings. Dialogue is balanced with exposition. This means that crucial information doesn't always have to be spoken aloud by characters. Instead, it can be integrated into the narrative prose.

A screenplay relies on visual and auditory experiences. In contrast, novels use all senses. The reader can experience what a character smells in an old library, how the chill of a snowy evening feels against their skin, or the taste of a long-awaited meal.

Since you have no budget, big scenes, settings, and action are limitless. A world that, in a film, would require expensive sets or CGI, can now be a dazzling setting.

While a screenplay provides a story blueprint, a novel allows for an expansive mansion to be built on that foundation. By understanding the core structure and beats of your screenplay, you can flesh out the story, crafting a novel that keeps the heart of your original idea.

Ironically, once you have a book version of your project, you have a sales tool to sell your screenplay and hopefully get the movie made. A novel gives your screenplay instant cachet, opening doors to producers, directors, and actors.

This book guides you through the process of turning your screenplay into a novel. Given your background in storytelling, we'll skip the basics and dive straight into the nitty-gritty.

Are you ready to embark on this exciting journey? Let's jump in and turn your screenplay into the novel it's meant to be.

Part One: Getting Ready to Write

Welcome to the thrilling adventure of transforming your screenplay into a novel! This section is your launchpad. Here, I'll lay the groundwork for turning your cinematic script into a rich, nuanced novel that will captivate readers and transport them into the world you have created.

As you transition from screenplay to novel, you're not just writing a longer version of your story; you are building a new, immersive experience. This section is all about preparing you for this transformation, setting you up with the tools, mindset, and inspiration you will need to make this leap with confidence and creativity. Besides looking at your story with a new perspective, you will set the stage for your book's success by growing an audience of eager readers as you are writing.

Buckle up and get ready to embark on this exciting journey! By the end of this section, you'll be fully equipped, inspired, and eager to dive into novel writing. Let's make your screenplay's transition into a novel an unforgettable adventure, filled with creativity, growth, and storytelling magic!

Step 1: Read in Your Genre

> Get ready to dive into the exciting world of genre! In this step, you'll immerse yourself in the top books of your chosen genre, discovering the nuances and styles that make these stories shine. We'll explore how to identify your subgenre, understand reader expectations, and learn from the best in the business. Let's get reading!

Before you start, and while you are working on your novel adaption, read as many books in your genre as you can. Reading is an easy way to learn the prose writing style used in your type of story. Read the current and long-time bestsellers. The best place to find a list is Amazon's Top 100 in your genre and subgenre.

For those new to writing fiction, immersing yourself in books from your chosen genre is invaluable. This practice is crucial to learning and improving your fiction writing. While you don't want to mimic another author's style, seeing how other authors write will help you develop your unique voice.

Just as important as your broad genre (action adventure), is figuring out your subgenre (spy thriller). Get specific as possible. Understanding your subgenre is crucial to refining your storytelling and reaching your target audience effectively. You will use your subgenre when listing your book on Amazon and on other online platforms. Online, you will use genres, subgenres, and their associated keywords to help readers find you.

Subgenres for Authors

Definition: A subgenre is a more specific category within a broader genre. Genres are large, general categories of literature like Romance, Science

Fiction, or Fantasy. Subgenres break these down further, focusing on particular themes, settings, or stylistic elements.

Why Are Subgenres Important?

- **Target Audience:** Subgenres help you connect with a more targeted group of readers, finding your audience. These people will be interested in buying and reading your book and hopefully become fans.

- **Literary Expectations:** Each subgenre comes with its own set of expectations and tropes, which can guide your writing.

- **Marketing:** You market and sell to readers that like your subgenre and are more likely to buy your book.

- **Shelving:** Books are shelved (both online and in real life) according to their subgenre, making it easier for readers to find them.

Examples of Subgenres:

1. Science Fiction

- Cyberpunk: Focuses on the intersection of high tech and low life, often featuring advanced technology and cybernetics.

- Space Opera: Emphasizes romantic, often melodramatic, adventure set mainly or entirely in outer space.

2. Fantasy

- Epic Fantasy: Involves epic stories set in a fictional universe, often with a medieval feel.

- Urban Fantasy: Incorporates magical elements into a modern, urban setting.

3. Romance

- Historical Romance: Set in a specific historical period, often involving real people.

- Paranormal Romance: Involves romantic relationships where one or both of the partners are supernatural beings.

4. Mystery

- Cozy Mystery: Violence and crime are downplayed or treated humorously. Often set in a small community.

- Hard-boiled: Features tough, unsentimental detectives and gritty realism.

Tip: Understand tropes. Familiarize yourself with the common tropes and expectations within your chosen subgenre.

Genre and tropes help you meet the reader's expectations. Happy readers mean more sales.

While You Are Reading Notice:

How Authors Handle:

- Point of view (POV) characters
- Internal monologue
- Language and writing style
- Pacing

The Book Covers:

- What do the covers in your genre look like?
- Fonts
- Color schemes
- Images

Examples of Writing Styles Within Genres:

1. Narrative Techniques: Different genres use specific narrative techniques. For example, mystery novels rely heavily on suspense and foreshadowing, while romance focuses more on character relationships and dialogue. Reading widely in your genre will help you pick up valuable techniques.

2. Vocabulary and Language Use: Each genre has its own lexicon and style. Fantasy uses more elaborate, descriptive language, while thrillers often have a terse, fast-paced style.

Immersing yourself in books of your chosen genre is a step you cannot afford to skip. To refine your writing style, reading within your genre is an indispensable part of becoming a successful novelist. Remember, every book you read not only enhances your understanding of the genre, but also fuels your inspiration and growth as a writer.

Take Aways

1. Reading in your genre will help you improve your prose.

2. You can learn a lot about writing craft and book covers by reading in your genre.

3. Get specific about your subgenre.

4. Genres help in writing, marketing, and selling your book.

Action Steps

1. Check Amazon for the current bestsellers in your genre.

2. Read as many as you can.

Step 2: Read Your Screenplay

> 👣 It's time to revisit your screenplay with fresh eyes! In this step, I'll guide you through the process of rediscovering your story, identifying its strengths and weaknesses, and envisioning its potential as a novel. You will analyze what you love and what might need a tweak. Get ready to fall in love with your characters and story all over again!

Read your screenplay. If it is an old script, it's probably been a while since you thought of it. You might even have forgotten some of the key elements.

Read it as if the story is brand new to you, thinking about how you would turn it into a book.

Notice what you like and don't like about it.

- Are there scenes that you want to cut?
- Are there places you would like to expand?
- Which character's story is it?
- Who is your favorite character?
- Is there a character who seems like the natural narrator?
- Are there missing tropes you would like to add?

Take Aways

1. Read your screenplay to get refamiliarized with your story.

Action Steps

1. Read your screenplay, noticing what you like and don't like about it.

2. Make notes about things you would like to change and add.

Step 3: Write a Scene Breakdown

👣 In this step, you will learn how to create a detailed scene breakdown that will serve as your road map for the adaptation process. Now comes the fun part: breaking down your screenplay scene by scene! You'll decide what stays, what goes, and what needs a little extra magic. Think of this step as crafting the perfect blueprint for your novel, setting the stage for an epic transformation. Get ready to dissect your story and uncover its hidden gems!

Adapting a screenplay into a novel is a journey of reimagining and transformation. While it's tempting to believe adaptation is a direct transfer of scenes from one medium to another, there is more to it. Recognizing what to keep, what to let go of, and what to add is at the core of this metamorphic process.

Think of your screenplay as a detailed outline for your novel. By analyzing each scene, you can decide which ones to flesh out further, which ones to condense, and what to add.

Understanding what exists in the screenplay is just the starting point. The real magic lies in this new vision, ensuring that the spirit of the story remains intact while it finds a new, expansive expression as a novel.

Steps in a Scene Breakdown

1. List each scene. Start by listing each scene in your screenplay with a logline.

2. What is the purpose? Identify the primary purpose of each scene. Does it advance the plot? Introduce or develop a character? Establish a setting or mood?

3. What is the emotional impact? Consider the emotional weight of each scene. Does it have a major revelation? A turning point for a character? A climax or resolution for a subplot? Highlight these key moments. They are the anchors of your story, and they might need more space and depth in a novel.

4. Character presence and development. Note which characters are in each scene and how they change throughout the story.

5. Cut and add scenes. While the scene breakdown process is about understanding what exists in the screenplay, it's also about recognizing what can be added or subtracted. Not every scene will be necessary for the novel. Conversely, there will be new scenes or moments that can enhance the story in this more expansive format.

Cut and add scenes in both your scene breakdown and your screenplay, so that they are up to date and match. For new scenes, just add a slugline and a logline. This will come in handy later when you convert your screenplay into a novel format.

Ways to Improve Scenes

1. Cutting Scenes When embarking on an adaptation, it's essential to look critically at each scene and ask: Does this scene serve the story in the novel format? Sometimes, the answer might be no. For example, in a screenplay, a montage sequence quickly conveys the progression of time. In a novel, a montage could feel jarring. Instead, a writer might choose to detail one or two poignant moments from the montage, diving deeper into the character's experiences and emotions.

2. Adding Scenes: In novels, there are no budgets. The only limit is the writer's imagination. Scenes which were too complicated and expensive for the screenplay can be in the novel. This is a chance to write your dream scenes. Consider moments in the screenplay characters make decisions that change the course of the plot. In the screenplay, these decisions are shown through action. In the novel, a new scene can take readers into the whirlwind of the character's thoughts. Subplots and backstories can be fleshed out in the novel, adding layers to the story.

3. Scenes that Reveal Character: Some of the most compelling scenes may not be action-packed or plot-heavy but instead offer a deep dive into a character's psyche. Scenes that provide a glimpse into a character's history, motivations, fears, and dreams are invaluable. They can be expanded upon, offering readers a richer understanding of the characters' world.

4. Character Arcs: You probably already have your character arcs mapped out. If not, chart the journey for each main character. Where do they begin emotionally, mentally, and physically? Where do they end? What are the key moments of change? By understanding the trajectory of your characters in the screenplay, you can identify where more depth, background, or internal reflection might be beneficial in the novel.

With this road map of the new scene breakdown and analysis, you have an outline to craft a novel that not only stays true to the screenplay's heart but also explores new territories of emotion, depth, and storytelling.

Take Aways

1. Writing a scene breakdown helps you analyze your script.

2. Focus on what to cut and add.

3. In a novel you can expand:

- Subplots

- Backstories

- Character arcs

Action Steps

1. Write a scene breakdown, including the logline, characters, purpose, and emotional impact.

2. If you decide to cut scenes, cut them out of both the screenplay and scene breakdown.

3. If you decide to add scenes, add them to the screenplay and scene breakdown with a slugline and logline. This keeps both documents current and will be helpful when you convert the screenplay into novel format.

Step 4: Build Your Email List

> 👣 Building an email list is like gathering a group of your biggest fans all in one place! Creating an email list is your golden ticket to connecting directly with your audience. We'll explore ways to entice subscribers and keep them eagerly anticipating your book's release. In this step, I will share the secrets to creating an irresistible reader magnet and crafting newsletters that will keep your readers engaged and excited. Get ready to connect with your audience and build a loyal following!

Email Newsletters

One essential aspect of indie publishing is an email newsletter. It is a powerful tool in an author's arsenal for building a connection with readers. As a writer, your email list is one of your most valuable assets. It's a direct line to your readers and potential readers.

What are Email Newsletters and Why Do You Need One?

Email newsletters are emails sent regularly to a list of subscribers who have opted-in to receive news from you. They can include updates about your writing, exclusive previews, personal anecdotes, and more.

The best thing you can do to set yourself up for success as a novelist is to start building your email list, and writing and sending newsletters while you are writing your book. That way, when you are ready to publish, you have a list of interested and eager buyers.

Why are Email Newsletters So Important?

1. Direct Communication: Unlike social media algorithms, which are always changing, email newsletters ensure direct communication with your audience. Social media platforms come and go in popularity and influence (I'm looking at you Twitter), but email is forever.

2. You Control Your List: You own your email list. With social media, you can lose your account, or an app can go out of business, and then you have no way to reach your followers. All of that hard work building an audience goes up in smoke. With an email list, you have your readers' email addresses and can always contact them.

3. Build Relationships: Newsletters help you build lasting relationships with your readers by providing consistent, personal updates and an easy way for readers to interact directly with you.

4. Promote Your Work: Email newsletters are an excellent tool for selling your books to readers by promoting new releases, book signings, and sales.

How to Grow Your Email List

Everyone starts at zero with their newsletter subscribers. The first thing to do is to ask your family and friends to subscribe. Then it's time to start growing your list with people you don't know, but who are potential readers.

1. Use a Reader Magnet: Attract subscribers by offering a free piece of writing related to your book in return for their email address. (More on what a reader magnet is shortly.)

2. Your Website: Add a subscription form on your website where you offer the reader magnet. (More on websites in a minute.)

3. Newsletter Swaps: Use services like BookFunnel and Story Origin for newsletter swaps where you can send your reader magnet to other authors' lists.

4. Referral Services: On ConvertKit's Creator Network and SparkLoop, other newsletter creators recommend yours.

5. Engage on Social Media: Promote your reader magnet on social media.

What Do I Write About?

Your newsletters don't have to be long. A few hundred words; just a couple of paragraphs. Subscribe to your favorite authors' newsletters for ideas.

1. Fun content related to your book. For example, if your book takes place in 1930s San Francisco, you can write a few newsletters about how much the city has changed.

2. Recommend books in your genre.

3. Recommend movies and television shows in your genre.

4. Personal updates related to your book, like research trips.

5. Updates on your writing progress.

How Often Should I Send My Newsletter?

The key is regularly connecting with your audience. Once a month is fine.

Do I Really Have to Start a Newsletter?

Yes. Successful authors have newsletters, even traditionally published ones.

What Tools Do I Need to Send a Newsletter?

You can't use Gmail or Outlook to send out mass emails. You will need an email marketing service to send your newsletter. There are many services out there to choose from. I use and recommend ConvertKit. ConvertKit and MailerLite both have free plans until you reach a thousand subscribers. Substack is always free. All of these choices let you write and schedule emails ahead of time. (By the way, the goal is to quickly grow your list to over a thousand people. The more subscribers you have, the more customers you have.)

The difference between Substack and other services is that it only has newsletters. Email marketing services like ConvertKit offer two big tools:

1. **Email automation** lets you design email sequences to be sent automatically. The most common is a welcome sequence to new subscribers.

2. **Segmenting** lets you send certain emails to certain people. For example, sending to subscribers in your hometown to tell them your books are available in the local bookstore. You can segment your email list based on reader interests and send tailored content to each group.

For indie authors, an email newsletter is more than just a marketing tool; it's a bridge connecting you to your readers. By growing your email list and maintaining regular, meaningful contact with your subscribers, you build a community of dedicated readers. Writers can build a stronger connection with their audience, promote their work more effectively, and ultimately sell more books.

By nurturing your email list, when your novel is ready to launch, email automation becomes a powerful promotional tool. You can schedule a series of emails leading up to the launch, sharing behind-the-scenes content, sneak peeks of your book, and special offers. This builds anticipation and can lead to more sales upon release.

To build your list, you will need a reader magnet. In the world of indie publishing, a reader magnet can be a powerful tool in your marketing arsenal. It helps in building a mailing list, enhances reader engagement, and serves as an effective introduction to your writing.

What is a Reader Magnet?

A reader magnet is a free piece of writing offered by an author to potential readers in exchange for their email address. This can be a short story or a novella that introduces your novel's premise, characters, and setting to readers.

Why Are Reader Magnets Important?

1. Building Your Mailing List: Offering a reader magnet helps in gathering email addresses, which is vital for building your mailing list.

2. Building Your Audience: It provides an opportunity to engage with your audience, entice them to become interested in your story, and attract new readers.

How to Write a Reader Magnet

Think bonus content. Your reader magnet can be a short story or novella that takes place before your novel. It can be a character's backstory or even a scene or two right before your story starts. It is the perfect appetizer for your novel to get your readers excited.

Even though it's free, your reader magnet should be well written and engaging. You are introducing your writing to new readers, so it is important to make a good first impression. It should make readers want more, leading them to buy your novel.

To look professional, your reader magnet will need a cover that is consistent with your genre (See Step 12). To save money at this stage, you can DIY a cover. However, I do not recommend going the DIY route for your book. This cover can be a placeholder that you swap for a better cover later that has some of the same elements (cover and font) as your completed book.

How Do You Get Your Reader Magnet to Your Readers?

BookFunnel and Story Origin are easy-to-use services that let authors distribute their digital books via email. Readers get an autogenerated email with their book attached and instructions on how to load it onto their e-readers. Both services create landing pages (one page websites) for reader magnets and books, and offer newsletter swaps to grow your email lists. By using a service like BookFunnel or Story Origin, you can ensure a smooth and professional experience for your readers, which is essential in building a loyal audience.

Take Aways

1. Email newsletters are a critical part of marketing your book, growing your fan base, and staying in touch with readers.

2. You will need an email marketing service like ConvertKit, MailerLite, or Substack to send your newsletters.

3. A reader magnet is a bonus short story or novella connected to your story world that you use to promote your book and collect emails to grow your list.

4. You can use Story Origin or BookFunnel to send your reader magnet to readers and grow your mailing list with newsletter swaps.

Action Steps

1. Write your reader magnet.

2. Choose an email marketing service. I recommend ConvertKit and MailerLite.

3. Sign up for BookFunnel or Story Origin to deliver your reader magnet and participate in newsletter swaps to grow your list.

4. Add your friends and family to your email list.

5. Start promoting your reader magnet to get subscribers.

Step 5: Build Your Website

> Your website is like your virtual home on the internet, and I'm here to help you make it cozy and inviting! A simple, effective website will showcase your writing, promote your book, and connect you with readers. In this step, I'll walk you through the process of creating a website. Let's get you set up in a cozy corner on the Internet where your fans can always find you.

The most effective way to market yourself and your writing is a website that explains who you are, what you do, what you have done, and how to get in touch with you.

Your website doesn't need to be complicated. It can be one page that you add to as needed. You can build and maintain your own website, even if you aren't techie. If I can do it, you can do it.

I built my website on WordPress. WordPress started off as a blogging platform, and now 60% of websites are built using WordPress. For search engine optimization (SEO) WordPress sites rank much higher than sites built on Wix, Weebly, or Squarespace.

When you build on WordPress, you choose a theme, which is the architecture for your website. I use the Divi theme because it offers lots of design possibilities and it's very easy to use. On your website you use plugins, which are like apps. ConvertKit has a plugin which lets you include a pop up form so that people can easily subscribe to your newsletter when they visit your site.

You will need a domain name and web hosting. I suggest using your name or something similar like yournamewrites.com. I use and recommend SiteGround for domains and hosting. Their tech support is amazing. They only work with WordPress sites, so if you have trouble with WordPress, they will help you with that too.

Use your site to promote your screenwriting, your book, and all of your creative projects. Be sure to include your contact info and your agent's (if you have one). You can sell e-books directly from your website using BookFunnel or Story Origin. When you sell directly to your readers, you keep all the money. Also, you can link to your book on Amazon and other online retailers. Be sure to sign up for an Amazon Associate account so that you get affiliate money when your website visitors click through to Amazon.

Two other book promotional tools to include are book club questions and a reading order if you have a series of books.

AuthorMedia.com has a free course "How to Make Your Author Website Amazing," that walks you through building your WordPress site with Divi in a day.

Take Aways

1. You need a website to promote your books, screenplays, and creative projects.

2. You can build your website yourself using WordPress.

Action Steps

1. Buy a domain.

2. Sign up for web hosting on a service like SiteGround for WordPress sites.

3. Install WordPress on your site.

4. Pick and install your theme. (I recommend Divi.)

5. Watch Authormedia.com's course "How to Make Your Author Website Amazing" and build your site.

6. Add your contact information.

7. Add an email subscriber form to your website to grow your email list.

8. Sell your books directly on your website.

9. Add buy button links to all the online retailers.

Step 6: Choose Your POV

> Choosing your novel's point of view (POV) is like trying on different pairs of glasses until you find the perfect fit! Step into your characters' shoes and see the world through their eyes! In this step, we'll explore the various POV options. Get ready to see your story from a whole new perspective!

Getting Inside Your Characters' Heads: Internal Monologue

With prose, you can experience a character's thoughts and emotions. This is called the internal monologue. This tool offers a direct line into a character's mind, allowing readers to experience their unique, personal perspective.

When we watch a film, a talented actor conveys a wealth of emotion through their performance. The audience must interpret what's going on inside a character's mind based on their words, actions, and behaviors. As readers, we are privy to a character's inner monologue, their hidden emotions, and their unspoken fears and desires.

Novel characters' internal world of thoughts, emotions, memories, and perception shape their behavior. This inner monologue gives the reader a behind-the-scenes glimpse into a character's mind.

Different Ways to Use Internal Monologue

1. Contradiction: A character's thoughts often contradict their behavior, revealing inner conflict, hidden desires, or concealed emotions. Thoughts can contrast a character's public facade with their private self, their actions with their intentions, their spoken words with their unspoken thoughts.

2. Build tension: Characters contemplate their circumstances, speculate about future events, or grapple with decisions. These internal deliberations can hint at future developments, create suspense, or sow the seeds for plot twists.

3. Readers connect with characters: Readers don't just observe events; they also experience characters' emotions. This shared experience creates a deep emotional bond between readers and characters—the reader is with the character, experiencing events in real-time. Harnessing this power of emotional engagement and empathy is key to creating a story that resonates deeply with readers.

4. Balance: Too much inner monologue can slow down the pace, boring the reader. It's crucial to balance showing and telling, action and reflection. The inner monologue should not replace action or dialogue but complement them to create a well-rounded story.

5. Character's Voice: The style and voice of the inner monologue should always reflect the character's personality, background, and mood. For example, a teenager's thoughts will be different from an elderly person's. A character will think differently when they're calm than when they're stressed.

As you transition your screenplay into a novel, mastering the art of the inner monologue will be an important new skill.

Choose Your POV: A Buffet of Options

The internal monologue works hand-in-hand with the point of view (POV) character who narrates a story in a novel. In a screenplay, the point of view is usually omniscient, observing all the characters equally. (The exception is screenplays with voice over.) However, in a novel, the point of view is that of the character (or characters) through whom we are experiencing the story.

The point of view that you choose for your novel will significantly influence the tone, style, and depth of emotion. The three most common points of view are: first person, third person omniscient, and limited third. Each has their strengths and weaknesses. There is no right or wrong answer; you must decide which point of view works best for you and your story.

The first step in choosing a point of view is deciding who your main character will be. Whose story do you want to tell? If you are unsure of which POV would work best, try writing the same scene in the three points of view: first person, third person omniscient, and limited third.

First-Person Narration

1. Narrated by a Character: A character narrates the story using I and me pronouns. We experience everything from their perspective and the story is told in their voice, which adds flavor and tone.

2. Limited Perspective: This approach confines the story to the perspective of one character, restricting access to other characters' thoughts and limiting scenes to those experienced by the character narrator. In other words, you can only have scenes that the narrator character is in.

3. Unreliable Narrator: Authors can use the technique of an unreliable narrator, where we are not sure if characters are telling us the truth. For example, Amy in *Gone Girl* by Gillian Flynn is the quintessential unreliable narrator as we slowly find out she has engineered her disappearance to frame her husband for her murder.

4. Immersive Internal World: This approach offers an immersive look into the internal world of the protagonist, as seen in *The Hunger Games* by Suzanne Collins. Katniss Everdeen's internal thoughts, feelings, and reactions to the brutal world around her bring high emotional stakes to the story.

Two Types of Third Person POV

In third person point of view (POV) the story is told from an outside perspective, referring to characters using third person pronouns like he, she, or they. Within third person POV, there are two variations that determine how intimately the reader is acquainted with a character's thoughts, feelings, and knowledge. They are **third person omniscient** and **third person limited**. Here is a breakdown of their differences.

Third Person Omniscient

1. The All-Knowing Narrator: The narrator knows everything about all characters – their thoughts, feelings, histories, and futures. They are not limited by time, place, or character.

2. Narrative Voice: Often, the voice of the narrator is more pronounced in this style, and they might provide commentary on events or characters, guiding the reader's perceptions.

3. Multiple Perspectives: Since the narrator is omniscient, the story can dive into the thoughts and feelings of multiple characters. Character POV can switch from section to section or chapter to chapter. Bonnie Garmus uses multiple perspectives in *Lessons in Chemistry*. There is even a chapter from the dog's POV.

4. Advantage: This POV allows for comprehensive world-building and a broader understanding of multiple characters' motivations and feelings. It can create a more sweeping and epic feel to the story.

5. Challenge: It can sometimes be overwhelming for readers if there are too many characters' POVs. Limiting the numbers of characters using POV and putting the character's names as chapter titles can help avoid confusion.

Third-Person Limited

This POV mode balances the subjective view of first person and the objective view of third person omniscient. In third person limited narration, the story focuses on one character, offering access to their thoughts and feelings while describing events.

For instance, in J. K. Rowling's Harry Potter series, the story is in third person limited, focusing on Harry's perspective. The story explores Harry's thoughts and emotions while maintaining a third-person viewpoint, allowing readers to connect with Harry on an emotional level while also providing a broader view of the story.

1. Limited Insight: As the name suggests, this POV is limited to the thoughts, feelings, and perceptions of one character. The reader gains intimate knowledge of this character, but only external observations of others.

2. Deep Connection: Since readers are privy to one character's internal world, they form a deeper connection to that character.

3. Narrative Voice: In third person limited, the narrative voice tends to align closely with the character's voice. The descriptions, observations, and tone often reflect the character's personality, education, and emotional state.

4. Advantage: This POV offers a focused and immersive experience, allowing readers to walk in the shoes of the character, experiencing their challenges, triumphs, and emotions firsthand.

5. Challenge: Since the story is bound by one character's knowledge and perspective, the author must find creative ways to introduce information or events outside of the POV character's direct experience—just like first person POV.

Common POV Pitfalls to Avoid

1. Over-Internalization: Consider whether the same information could be conveyed through dialogue or action. Often, showing a character's emotional state through their actions can be more powerful than simply telling the reader what the character is feeling.

2. Head-Hopping: It's important to maintain a consistent narrative focus on one character's thoughts and feelings at a time. Switching too rapidly or without clear transitions between different characters' perspectives—a mistake known as head-hopping—can confuse the reader.

3. Telling Instead of Showing: Remember to balance telling with showing. Show your characters' feelings through their actions, dialogue, interactions with others, and their reactions to events.

Alternating POVs by Chapter

Switching between points of view in alternating chapters is a popular technique in novel writing. By switching between characters' POVs, you can give the audience a full view of the story, instead of being limited to one character's experience.

How to Alternate POVs

1. Distinct Character Voices: When you alternate between characters, it's essential that each one has a unique voice. This means they have distinct speech patterns in dialogue, but also that their thoughts and narrative style reflect their unique personalities.

For example, a street-smart detective might have a sharp, no-nonsense way of interpreting the world, while a dreamy poet might view the same setting with a flood of emotions and a touch of whimsy. As readers navigate between chapters, these unique voices offer different aspects of the story.

2. Limit your POVs: While it's tempting to hop into the minds of many characters, it is usually beneficial to limit the POVs to two or three. Too many can confuse readers.

3. Signposting: It should be immediately clear whose perspective the reader is experiencing when they start a new chapter. Label chapters with the POV character's name and sometimes the time and setting. Chapter titles can be similar to slug lines in a screenplay, anchoring the reader to a time, place, and character.

4. Using POV to Control Pacing: Alternating POVs can be a powerful tool to control the story's pacing. If one character's arc is reaching a climax, switching to another character can create a cliffhanger, keeping readers eager to continue.

5. Handling Time: When switching between POVs, it's essential to keep track of the timeline. Does each chapter occur simultaneously? Does one character's story lag behind another? Clear markers, whether explicit like dates at the beginning of chapters or implicit, referencing shared events, can help keep readers oriented.

Take Aways

1. The internal monologue is how the reader experiences the main character's thoughts and emotions.

2. The style and voice of the inner monologue should reflect the character's personality, background, and mood.

3. The three most common points of view are: first person (I), third person omniscient (he/she), and limited third (he/she).

4. You can have more than one POV character by alternating chapters.

5. When alternating POV, it is good practice to put the character's name in the chapter title.

Action Steps

1. Try writing the same scene in the three points of view: first person, third person omniscient, and limited third.

2. Choose which POV to use.

3. Consider using alternating POVs.

Step 7: Converting Your Screenplay Into Prose with Scrivener

> 👣 Meet your new best friend, Scrivener! This powerful tool will make converting your screenplay into novel format a breeze. In this step, I'll guide you through the process of importing your script and reorganizing your scenes. Get ready to organize, write, and edit

> like a pro, turning your script into a beautifully crafted book.

Introduction to Scrivener

As working screenwriters, you may not have heard of Scrivener. It is word processing software designed for long form writing projects and used by most novelists. This book was written in Scrivener!

In Microsoft Word, you have one long document, which makes it difficult to move sections around because you may have to scroll for a long time to find your place. It's easy to get confused and cut and paste text in the wrong place or accidentally delete something. In contrast, Scrivener mimics a physical binder with folders and documents that you can see all at once. It is easy to move sections around by simply dragging and dropping.

While MS Word has been a stalwart for word processing, Scrivener triumphs in meeting the needs of novelists. From the beginning stage of organizing ideas, developing characters, and outlining plots, to the final phases of revising and preparing manuscripts for publication, Scrivener stands out as a comprehensive, author-centric tool.

The convenience, functionality, and writer-friendly design of Scrivener undeniably make it the best choice for novelists.

Let's get into the specifics of how Scrivener stands out as a powerful tool that enhances the process of novel writing, overshadowing the conventional utility of MS Word.

1. Story Organization

- **The Binder:** Scrivener's binder enables writers to manage their manuscript in chunks, which can be entire chapters, scenes, or even smaller fragments. This flexibility in managing the narrative structure is absent in Word, which offers a linear and unbroken writing and scrolling experience.

- **Corkboard View:** Scrivener's corkboard view will be familiar to screenwriters. Each scene or chapter is represented by a virtual index card, enabling authors to visually organize their narratives with easy drag-and-drop functionality.

2. Character and Plot Development Tools

- **Character Sheets**: provide space for you to create detailed character bios, where you can store vital information about each character's traits, arcs, and development. This allows for easy reference without the need to open a new document or window.

- **Plot Outlining:** Scrivener's outlining tools facilitate the skillful development and tracing of plot points, twists, and resolutions.

3. Research at Your Fingertips

- **Research Folder:** Unlike Word, Scrivener boasts a dedicated space to store all your research. Whether it's images, PDFs, documents, or web pages, you can keep all your materials within one project in Scrivener for easy access, without having to toggle between applications.

- **Split Screen View:** The split-screen feature allows writers to view their research or notes side-by-side with their writing, eliminating the need to switch windows.

- **Keep:** Screenplay notes and earlier drafts are easy to access.

4. Manuscript Formatting Tailored to Authors' Needs

- **Preset and Customizable Templates:** Scrivener comes with templates for novels or you can customize your own.

- **Compiling for Publication:** Scrivener's compile feature is incredibly helpful. You can transform your manuscript into various formats, like ePub (for digital books), Word, and PDF, and export seamlessly. This function makes it easy to upload your book to online stores.

5. Extensive Revision Tools

- **Snapshot Feature:** Before starting on revisions, Scrivener's snapshot tool allows you to save versions of scenes or chapters, enabling you to make changes without the fear of losing previous versions. Snapshots take a "picture" of your document at a particular point, allowing you to easily revert to previous versions.

- **Experiment**: With scenes or characters without the fear of losing the original text.

- **Compare Different Versions:** of a scene or chapter to select the one that fits best.

- **Revision Mode:** While Word has the Track Changes feature, Scrivener's Revision Mode allows for layered revisions, each in a different color or label, so you can see where you are in your story.

6. Target Setting to Guide Your Writing

- **Writing Goals:** Scrivener lets you set project and session targets, aiding you in managing your writing goals and maintaining a consistent writing pace. If you like to set daily word count goals, this feature will help you track them.

- **Statistics and Progress:** View your writing history to observe the progression and development of your project. With this data, you will see that you are making progress, which will make you want to write more.

The Binder Basics

The Binder is the heart of Scrivener, where authors can seamlessly house, maneuver, and manage every fragment of their story universe. Unlike Word, where a document is a continuous, linear flow of text, Scrivener's binder allows you to see your project from a bird's-eye view. This ensures that every piece of the manuscript, such as scenes, chapters, or parts, can be easily arranged, reassessed, and rearranged without disrupting the flow of creativity.

- **Effortlessly Rearranging Scenes and Chapters:** The intuitive interface of the

Binder allows users to shuffle scenes and chapters effortlessly, which is pivotal during editing.

- **Drag-and-Drop Functionality:** Say you've written a scene that fits better in chapter three than chapter one. With Scrivener, you simply click on the scene within the Binder, drag it up or down, and drop it into its new location. There's no need to cut and paste large chunks of text, avoiding potential errors or misplacements.

- **Hierarchical Structure:** The Binder lets you create parent and child documents, folders and subdocuments to maintain a clear structure of your manuscript. Chapters (parent documents or folders) can house multiple scenes (child documents), and any changes in the hierarchy, like moving a scene from one chapter to another, are done with simple dragging and dropping.

- **Global Overview:** Scrivener presents an unbridled view of your entire project, showcasing chapters, scenes, and even your research, all in a single window. This global perspective helps maintain consistency in plot development, ensuring that story threads are followed through and character arcs are developed cohesively.

- **Accessibility:** The Binder keeps every element of your novel - from various scenes and chapters to character sheets and research - just a click away, eliminating the need to scroll through lengthy documents or toggle between windows. This ease of access ensures that writers can instantly navigate to different sections of their novel, enhancing efficiency and maintaining the flow of writing.

- **Color-Coding and Status:** Scrivener lets you assign colors and status stamps (such as First Draft, Revised, etc.) to various sections in the Binder. At a glance, you can understand where extra attention might be required or recognize the parts that have been finalized, optimizing the revision and editing processes.

As your story takes shape, changes, or takes unexpected turns, the Binder allows for real-time, instantaneous reorganization of your manuscript structure.

Scrivener's Binder isn't just a tool for organization; it's a dynamic, visual, and interactive representation of your narrative universe. The ability to manipulate, visualize, and navigate through this universe with such ease and precision is a powerful tool for novelists.

How to Import a Screenplay into Scrivener

Now that we have taken a tour of Scrivener, it's time to turn your screenplay into a novel. Here is a step-by-step guide on how to import a screenplay into Scrivener and reformat it into a novel:

Step 1: Importing a Screenplay into Scrivener

- **Create a New Project:** Open Scrivener. Go to File > New Project and select the Novel template. Give your project a name and choose a save location.

- **Import the Screenplay:** Go to File > Import > Import & Split. After you choose your screenplay, the drop down list will have the choice Scene Heading. Select Scene Heading and then click Import.

Step 2: Understanding the Initial Binder Structure

Upon import, Scrivener converts each scene of your screenplay into a separate document within the Binder.

- **Draft/Manuscript Folder:** This is where your screenplay scenes will be imported.

- **Scene Documents:** Each scene from your screenplay will be its own text document, titled by the scene heading (slugline).

Step 3: Reformatting the Screenplay to a Novel Format

- **Scene Heading:** Add more information to each scene heading (your former slugline) so you can tell at a glance what the scene is about.

Step 4: Reorganizing the Binder for Novel Structure

At first keep your screenplay structure. Use a folder for each act and turn each scene into a document.

- **New Folders:** Create new folders for each act.

- **Moving Scenes:** Drag and drop individual scene documents into their respective act folders. (Later, you will add chapter folders with scene documents.)

Step 5: Using Scrivener's Features for Story Development

Character and Plot Development:

- Create character sheets within the Binder.

Research and Notes:

- Make use of the Research folder to store relevant materials.

- Use document notes for scene-specific or chapter-specific notes, like who's in the scene or highlighting pivotal moments.

Take Aways

1. Scrivener is designed for writing long documents like novels.

2. The Binder structure makes it easy to drag and drop large pieces of prose.

3. You can keep your research, including your screenplay, in the research folder.

4. You can track your progress with colors and labels.

Action Steps

1. Import your screenplay into Scrivener.

Part Two: Writing Your Novel

Welcome to the heart of the adventure, intrepid storyteller! This is where the real magic happens as we transform your screenplay into a novel that readers will devour.

I'll explore how to turn your screenplay's dialogue into rich, layered prose; develop scenes with lush descriptions; and expand your story with exciting subplots. With these new skills, you'll transform bare bones scenes into immersive experiences that will pull readers in. Finally, I'll guide you on how to organize your scenes into chapters that flow seamlessly and keep readers hooked.

Let's get writing!

Step 8: Start With the Dialogue

> 👣 Dialogue is the secret ingredient that brings your characters to life! In this step, I'll teach you how to adapt your screenplay's dialogue into engaging conversations that reveal your characters' personalities, motivations, and conflicts. Let's get talking!

Dialogue in novels doesn't bear the same burden as in screenplays. While it is an essential tool in the novelist's kit, it doesn't have to carry the entire narrative on its shoulders.

In novels, dialogue works in tandem with narrative prose to tell the story. It can reveal character traits, advance the plot, and offer insight into the characters' motivations and emotions; but it does not need to work as economically as in a screenplay.

Internal monologue and exposition provide an added layer of context around dialogue in novels. For instance, a novelist can tell the reader about a character's inner thoughts and feelings, either before, during, or after they speak. This ability to dip in and out of a character's internal and external experiences uses description, exposition, and character introspection.

Here are some things to consider when transitioning dialogue from a screenplay to a novel:

Expanding Dialogue into Inner Monologue

In screenplays, a lot is left unsaid. Characters might hint at their feelings or thoughts through subtle actions or dialogue that relies heavily on subtext. A simple line like "I'm fine" in a screenplay can be expanded in a novel to capture a character's conflicting emotions, past experiences, or hidden desires.

How to Adapt Dialogue-Driven Scenes

When transitioning into a novel, think about how you can intersperse the dialogue with descriptive details and introspection. While the core conversation remains essential, the accompanying prose provides insight into character dynamics, backstory, and setting.

The Power of Silence

In screenplays, pauses in dialogue are palpable. They can be filled with tension and anticipation. In novels, writers can translate these silences into introspection or description. A pause in a conversation might be a chance for a character to recall a relevant memory or grapple with an internal conflict.

Maintaining the Essence and Pace

Dialogue-driven scenes, by nature, have a rhythm and momentum. It's essential to ensure that introspection doesn't stall this momentum. The internal monologue should be woven seamlessly into the dialogue, providing depth without becoming a distraction.

Adapting Dialogue to the Novel Format

Now you have to adapt your dialogue to the novel format. In books, we don't have the luxury of seeing who is talking. Instead, the reader knows who is talking in two ways: character voice and dialogue tags.

Each time a new character speaks, a new paragraph starts. This transition lets the reader know someone new has started speaking.

As a seasoned screenwriter, your character voices should be distinct. But in long exchanges or groups, the reader will occasionally need to know who is speaking. That is where dialogue tags come in.

As Jeff Elkins, author of *The Dialogue Doctor Will See You Now*, explains, dialogue tags serve three purposes:

    1. They identify who is speaking.

    2. They change how the reader hears dialogue.

    3. They provide emotional embellishment.

Dialogue tags are the "he said, she said" we see in prose. For variety, dialogue tags can include characters' names and vivid, active verbs.

Examples of verbs you can use in dialogue tags:

- Shouted
- Yelled
- Screamed
- Barked
- Snapped
- Sang
- Trilled
- Laughed
- Mumbled
- Whispered
- Growled
- Smirked

We think of dialogue tags at the end of sentences. "I've never read that book," he said.

But they can also be in the middle of a character's speech. "I've always wanted to go to Paris," Sarah said. "Imagine the view from the Eiffel Tower."

Notice the rhythm of these two examples. Dialogue tags at the end of sentences move the reader quickly to the next line. Using a tag in the middle of a character's line breaks up the dialogue, slowing down the read.

Body language, while silent, is another aspect of how characters communicate. Is a character anxiously shifting in her seat or smiling seductively? These actions tell us a lot and move the conversation along.

So now, we've got the variations of dialogue tags:

- No tags.
- He said (I said for first person POV).
- Character name said.
- Using active verbs instead of said.
- Using at the end of sentences.
- Using in the middle of a sentence.
- Adding body language to dialogue and tags.

Now, different teachers have different philosophies about dialogue tags. Some people say never use them. Some say use them all the time. I say it's somewhere in the middle of these two extremes. I suggest experimenting with dialogue tags to find the way that works the best for your story, POV, and genre.

Silent Dialogue: Body Language

Think about how you imagined the actors playing this scene in your screenplay. In a novel, you get to direct your characters so that the reader feels what they are feeling.

You can use body language to add layers to your scene in several ways.

1. **Contradiction:** A character's body language can contradict what they're saying. A character can sound strong but look weak because her hands are shaking.

2. **Unspoken feelings:** A longing look or touch of a hand can tell us a character is in love with another.

3. **Emphasis:** Body language can emphasize a line. "Where is she?" George said as he looked at his watch.

4. **Internal Monologue:** Your POV character can read and comment on others' body language in his internal monologue. George noticed Louis' swagger and thought, what a jerk.

How to Interweave Dialogue and Internal Monologue

1. Contrast Saying With Feeling: Spoken words can sometimes be deceptive, hiding true feelings or intentions. With internal monologue, writers can present the contrast between what a character says and what they genuinely feel.

2. Enhancing Tension and Conflict: The dichotomy between spoken and unspoken words can heighten suspense and intrigue.

3. Deepening Emotions: With the internal monologue novelists capture the POV character's emotions. Such introspection provides a deeper understanding of a character's emotional journey, connecting readers to characters.

4. Illuminating Backstory and Motivations: Internal monologues can offer glimpses into a character's past, subtly filling in backstory without resorting to overt exposition.

Merging spoken dialogue with internal monologue is one of the novel's most potent tools, offering readers an all-access pass into a character's psyche. It unveils the intricacies of human emotion, the battles between said and unsaid, and the multifaceted nature of interpersonal interactions.

Take Aways

1. Dialogue tags tell the reader who is speaking.

2. Adding body language to dialogue and tags

3. Dialogue is interwoven with internal monologue.

4. Dive into your characters' thoughts, feelings, and internal conflicts to enrich the story.

5. Body language is an important part of dialogue.

6. Variations of dialogue tags:

- No tags

- He said (I said for first person POV.)

- Character name said

- Using active verbs instead of said

- Using at the end of sentences

- Using in the middle of a sentence

Action Steps

Add dialogue tags to your first scene using the variations discussed. Spend some time on this scene, rewriting using different kinds of tags in different ways until you get a feel for what is going to work for your story.

1. Add dialogue tags to your lines of dialogue using said and other verbs.

2. Use character names and pronouns.

3. Experiment with when and how often you use tags.

4. Add body language.

5. Add your POV character's internal monologue. What are they thinking about? What are they worried about? What do they think about what the other characters are saying? Do they believe them?

Step 9: Add Detail

> Adding detail to your novel is like painting a vivid picture with words! Time to sprinkle some magic dust! In this step, we'll explore how to use descriptive language, sensory details, and world-building to immerse your readers in your story. Get ready to create a rich and captivating narrative that will keep your readers hooked!

You have converted your dialogue to prose using dialogue tags. You have added internal dialogue for your point of view characters. Now it is time to add the rest of the detail to your story. In this section, we are going to talk about the different ways to use prose in a novel.

Prose offers the background information readers need to fully understand a story. It provides context, backstories, and paints the world in which the story unfolds. Use it to:

1. Set the Scene: Exposition sets the stage. It describes settings, eras, and the world's general mood, from dystopian landscapes to idyllic small towns. Prose paints vivid, sensory-filled pictures of the setting.

2. Organic Descriptions: Instead of lengthy expositions, weave descriptions organically into action or dialogue. A character brushing snow off their coat is more engaging than a detached observation about the snowfall.

3. Sensory Engagement: Use all the senses in descriptions.

4. Detailed Action Sequences: Action sequences in scripts are concise because of visual emphasis. In prose, you can expand on these, providing blow-by-blow details, characters' internal reactions, or even slowing time down for detail.

5. Internal Thoughts and Feelings: Exposition allows writers to dive deep into a character's mind, exploring their innermost thoughts, fears, and desires.

6. Expand on Dialogue: In prose, you can expand conversations through internal monologue or narration.

7. Backstory: Not all history can be revealed through dialogue without feeling forced. With exposition, you can introduce past events that shape the present narrative. With the expanded real estate of prose, you can explore character histories, relationships, and arcs.

8. Flashbacks and Memories: Prose gives the flexibility to seamlessly weave in flashbacks, dreams, or memories.

9. Incorporate Subplots: Prose offers the space to include subplots that add layers to the story, enrich the main plot, and develop supporting characters.

10. Narrative Voice and Style: You can have a unique narrative voice, whether it's the voice of a character or an omniscient narrator. This voice can add personality, humor, and tone to the story.

Let's talk through three ways to use prose in more detail.

Setting the Scene in Novels

Unlike screenplays, where we can see what's happening, novels require a setting description each time the story changes location. This scene description grounds the reader, letting them know where they are in the story. When it comes to novels, setting the scene offers readers a chance to immerse themselves fully, living in the moment alongside the characters.

At the heart of every captivating story is a setting that comes alive in the reader's mind. Imagine the dark, oppressive atmosphere of Victorian London in Charles Dickens' novels, or the enchanting realm of Middle-Earth in J.R.R. Tolkien's tales. These settings are almost characters in their own right, influencing events, moods, and even characters' decisions.

Just as characters evolve, settings can too. Using setting changes, be it destruction, growth, or transformation, can mirror character arcs or plot progression, playing an important part in the story. Imagine the emotions settings can evoke. For instance, a city recovering after a war, a forest with seasons changing, or a house that decays over time.

Engaging the Senses

Sprinkling a few striking, specific, sensory details breathes life into a scene. The sound of rustling leaves, the scent of fresh bread from a nearby bakery, or the cold, uneven cobblestones beneath a character's feet make a scene more tactile and real. You don't have to describe every single thing about the scene. Instead, give just enough information so that readers can fill in the rest of the details with their imagination. Writers should weave in details organically, allowing them to complement the dialogue rather than compete with it.

A conversation in a Parisian café becomes far more than an exchange of words; it's a sensory experience. The texture of the wrought-iron table, the gentle hum of French conversations, the warmth of sunlight streaming through the leaves—these elements infuse the dialogue with depth, making the conversation more than just words on a page. A novel's strength lies in its ability to engage all five senses, enveloping the reader in a multi-sensory experience.

Sight: Describe not only what characters see but how they perceive it, how it makes them feel, and what memories or thoughts it evokes.

Sound: The crackle of a fire, the whisper of wind through the trees, or the rhythm of a city at rush hour bring the story's setting to life.

Touch: The feel of a rough bark under a character's fingers, the heat of a fire warming their skin, the comfort of a familiar blanket—these sensations can add to the characters' and readers' experience, helping readers feel what the characters are feeling.

Smell: The smell of a particular perfume can remind a character of a lost love, or the scent of fresh cookies can transport them back to their grandmother's kitchen. A smell can trigger memories and powerful emotions.

Taste: Obviously, taste is most useful in scenes set around meals and drinks. The taste of a home-cooked meal can evoke memories and emotions. A bitter medicine can foreshadow an obstacle. The bitterness of unsweetened coffee, the sweet tang of a fruit, or the richness of a chocolate cake can mirror the emotions of the dialogue.

By embracing the power of the senses, you can transform your screenplay into a multi-dimensional, vivid, and engaging novel.

Converting Action to Descriptive Prose

Screenplays consist of crisp, visual descriptions of a character's actions. When transitioning to a novel, these actions require more depth. Here are methods for elongating and detailing. In particular, using the senses can make action scenes more powerful.

1. The Power of Introspection

In the screenplay, when Jane walks into the library, we don't know what she's thinking. However, in a novel, her entrance becomes an opportunity for introspection.

As Jane stepped into the library, the familiar scent of aged paper and polished wood enveloped her. She hesitated for a moment, taking it all in, and then with a determined stride headed toward the back. There was a particular book she sought that might hold the answers she so desperately needed.

Here, not only is Jane's action described, but we're given a glimpse into her past, her emotions, and her purpose.

2. Elongating the Action

In screenplays, actions are concise because they're bound by the real-time restrictions of film. In contrast, novels can stretch a single moment. This stretching allows for a deeper exploration of the character's emotions, intentions, and surroundings.

Jane's fingers grazed the rows of books, each spine telling tales of authors past and worlds unexplored. She remembered the joy of turning each page, the thrill of stumbling upon a new idea. And then she found it - the book she was looking for. She pulled it out, the weight familiar in her hands, and carefully opened it, hoping to unlock its secrets.

3. The Significance of Surroundings

The setting can influence a character's actions.

The library, with its towering oak bookshelves and ornate lamps casting a golden hue, had always been Jane's sanctuary. The soft rustling of pages turning, whispers of students discussing their latest finds, and the distant ticking of the grand clock comforted her.

4. Infusing Emotion into Action

While a screenplay visually depicts a character's emotion through their expressions and body language, novels express feelings.

Jane's heart raced as she flipped through the book. Each page brought a mix of anticipation and dread. What if the answers weren't there? What if they were? Her fingers trembled slightly, a mix of excitement and fear, as she continued her search.

5. Enhancing with Sensory Details

Novels engage all the reader's senses, making actions more vivid.

The book's pages felt slightly coarse, worn from years of handling. The faint scent of musk and ink lingered. In the distance, a soft thud sounded as someone set down a book. The muted conversations were a low hum in the background.

6. Internal Reactions

In a novel, actions can be paired with the character's feelings. They are not just about what the characters do but how they feel, why they do it, and the world they inhabit.

As Jane read a particular passage, a chill ran down her spine. 'Could this be it?' she thought. Her mind raced, piecing together the clues with this newfound knowledge.

Using Descriptive Prose to Enhance Dialogue

The prose around your dialogue adds another level of meaning. For instance, a line like "I've been waiting for you" can take on different tones depending on the accompanying description. It could be a romantic reunion, an impatient rebuke, or a menacing threat, all based on the surrounding prose.

The fun of a novel is dialogue and exposition are not mutually exclusive. Characters can reflect internally as they converse. A character might say one thing, think another, and act completely differently.

Character Backstories

While a screenplay might offer hints to a character's past through dialogue or brief flashbacks, a novel lets you dive deeply into a character's history.

A well-crafted backstory can provide valuable insight into why characters behave the way they do, revealing motives, explaining quirks, and shedding light on relationships. This increased understanding lets readers connect more intimately with your characters, rooting for their victories, mourning their losses, and ultimately investing in their journeys.

Backstory works best when dripped out slowly, instead of being dumped all at once. Your characters' pasts are a mystery that the reader gradually uncovers, feeding suspense and tension.

Subplots

Subplots can add dramatic tension, provide comic relief, or offer moments of reflection. They enrich the main plot, adding dimension and depth to your story. In a novel, you have time to expand your subplots or add ones you had to cut from your screenplay.

Here's a guide on how to skillfully weave in these elements without overshadowing the primary plot.

1. Purpose

Subplots should:

- Offer different perspectives on the central conflict.
- Enhance our understanding of the main characters.
- Introduce tension or complications.

- Expand on the world or setting.

2. Place In the Main Story

Subplots shouldn't overshadow the main storyline. If a subplot begins to feel like it's taking on a life of its own, consider it for a new novel, or it could be a sign that the main plot needs more development.

3. Timing and Pacing

Subplots should not disrupt the momentum of the main story. A well-timed subplot can provide a breather from the primary plot's tension or amplify it, depending on the desired effect. Transitioning between the main plot and subplots should feel fluid.

4. Interconnectivity

To ensure subplots don't feel disconnected, they should intersect with the main plot at key points. This can be through shared events, side characters influencing the main narrative, or the protagonist getting involved in the subplot.

5. Growth and Resolution

Just like your main story, subplots should have a beginning, middle, and an end. These characters should also grow and develop. Just as the primary plot requires a resolution, so do your subplots.

Their resolution should either precede the main plot's climax or be woven into it, ensuring that the primary storyline remains the central focus until the end.

6. Limit the Number

Limit your subplots to maintain clarity and focus. Too many threads can make a story convoluted.

💡 Take Aways

Use prose to:

1. Set the scene.

2. Weave descriptions organically into action or dialogue.

3. Use all five senses in description.

4. Make action sequences detailed.

5. Explore characters' internal thoughts and feelings.

6. Expand on dialogue with internal monologue or narration.

7. Reveal backstory.

8. Add flashbacks and memories.

9. Add subplots.

10. Develop a distinctive narrative voice and style.

Subplots should:

1. Offer different perspectives on the central

conflict.

2. Enhance our understanding of the main characters.

3. Introduce tension or complications.

4. Expand on the world or setting.

5. Don't pull focus from the main storyline.

Action Steps

Use the Senses:

1. Go through your scene and add in all the senses. Explore the sensory experiences of your POV character. What emotions and memories do they evoke?

2. Describe the surroundings in your scene. What are the dominant colors, and what's the quality of light? Are there any significant landmarks or unique details that can anchor the scene? Does the setting bring up any emotions or memories?

3. Beyond the spoken words in your scene, what are the background sounds? How does a character react to a sound?

4. What does a character touch? What emotion does it invoke?

5. What are the smells in your scene? How do they make the character feel? Do they evoke any memories?

Add prose to an action sequence:

1. Add some introspection for your POV character. What are they thinking and feeling? Add their emotional reactions.

2. Elongate a moment by adding introspection, setting, and sensory details.

3. Add emotion. What is at stake here for your POV character?

4. Add setting and sensory details.

Write your characters' backstories that are part of your plot.

1. When should you reveal what?

2. Make a note of backstory tidbits in the notes section of the scenes, so you remember to include them.

What are your subplots?

1. How do they connect to the main story?

2. In the notes section of the scenes, put subplot reminders so you can track them.

Step 10: Building Your Novel's Structure With Chapters

> Structuring your novel with chapters is like building a beautiful house, one room at a time! Think of each chapter as a mini-movie scene packed with action, emotion, and intrigue. In this step, I'll show you how to organize your scenes into cohesive chapters

> that propel your story forward and keep your readers turning the pages past their bedtime.

Now that you have rewritten all of your screenplay scenes into prose and added new ones, it is time to put them in chapters. Before you do that, let's talk in broad strokes about chapters.

Why Chapters Are Important

Transitioning from the visual, action-based format of a screenplay to the prose-driven structure of a novel, the chapter becomes your new primary unit of narrative progression. As the building blocks of your novel's structure, chapters let the author break down the story into digestible sections for the reader. A chapter is a distinct segment of the story that usually contains multiple scenes or a significant event. Ideally, chapters should be short enough so they can be read in a few minutes before bed.

Much like scenes in a screenplay, every chapter should have its own internal tension and mini-arc with a beginning, middle, and end that feeds into the overall story. It might start by setting up a problem, follow the characters' efforts to deal with it, and conclude with some resolution, whether successful or not.

Each chapter should contribute to the story's progression, either by advancing the plot, deepening character development, or enriching the story's world. The content of a chapter is typically cohesive, centered on a particular event, conflict, or theme.

The beginning of a new chapter signals a shift or progression in the story. This might be a change in time, setting, perspective, or mood. A new chapter might begin when:

- A new day dawns.
- The characters move to a different location.
- The point of view switches from one character to another.
- A significant event shifts the story in a new direction.
- Time jumps either forward or backward.

Most importantly, chapters manage the pace of the story. Chapter breaks keep your readers reading or give them a place to put the book down. Chapters provide rhythm and structure, guiding the flow of the story. Transitions between them are crucial for maintaining narrative flow. A chapter should end on a cliffhanger full of suspense, leaving the reader desperate to find out what happens next. This is an effective way to keep readers turning the pages and maintain tension.

Pacing in a novel is about how quickly or slowly the readers move through the story, the frequency of action versus introspection, and the time spent on detail. Chapter breaks serve as an essential tool for managing this pacing. They're like the conductor's baton in an orchestra, controlling the rhythm, tempo, and dynamic range of the story.

Chapter titles help transitions by sometimes having the time, location, or POV character in the title. Chapter titles can provide hints or insights about the content of the chapter, sparking curiosity or adding layers of meaning.

The focus of each chapter will depend on the narrative point of view. In a first-person or third-person limited POV, each chapter will usually continue the same character's journey. In contrast, novels with multiple point-of-view characters shift focus between chapters, alternating perspectives to provide a multifaceted view of the story.

By strategically expanding and condensing scenes and effectively using chapter breaks, you can craft a novel that maintains the essence of your screenplay while providing a deeper, more immersive story experience.

Here are three ways to use scenes in chapters.

1. Expanding a Scene into a Chapter

Sometimes, a single scene from a screenplay might expand into a full chapter in a novel. This expansion could be because of the depth of the event taking place or the impact of the scene on the characters. For instance, a scene of confrontation in a screenplay might be a turning point in the characters' relationship. In the novel version, this scene could expand into an entire chapter, sharing the characters' internal reactions by exploring their backstory, their thoughts and emotions, and using sensory detail.

2. Putting Multiple Scenes into a Chapter

Several scenes from a screenplay can form a single chapter in a novel. This could happen when a series of brief scenes in the script have a shared focus or collectively serve a common narrative purpose. For example, a sequence of scenes showing a character's daily routine might be one chapter in a novel, capturing the essence of their day-to-day life.

If several scenes involve the same characters, occur in the same location, or revolve around a similar theme, grouping these scenes together into one chapter will maintain thematic coherence and continuity.

3. Rearranging Scenes

The order of scenes might also change in the transition from screenplay to novel. This rearrangement could serve various purposes, such as enhancing narrative suspense, exploring characters more deeply, or revealing information at a more appropriate moment in the novel. For instance, a flashback scene in a screenplay could be moved to the beginning of the novel to set up a character's backstory before introducing their present circumstances.

Take Aways

Each chapter contributes to the narrative progression by:

- Advancing the plot
- Deepening character development
- Enriching the world

A chapter centers on:

- An event
- Conflict
- Theme

A new chapter signals a shift in:

- Time
- Setting
- Mood
- POV

Chapter titles help ground the reader with:

- POV characters
- Place
- Time

Action Steps

1. Make Folders in your Binder. These will be your chapters.

2. Name your chapter folders. These can be placeholder names, so you don't get stuck on this step. Do not name them by numbers because you may move them later.

3. Drag your scenes into their new chapters.

Side Note: Turning TV Pilots Into Novels & Writing Series

> This approach also works for turning television scripts into novels. With a TV pilot, you are setting up a series. And your novel version of your pilot does the same thing, setting up a series of books.

In the indie publishing world, it is easier to make money from a series because you get what's called **read through**. People like the first book and they read all the way through the series, making you money with each book they buy.

This idea of converting a TV series into a book series is easiest to imagine with mysteries. Each mystery (whether an episode or a season) can translate into one book. But this concept can work for other kinds of television as well. Think of *Yellowstone* with each season being a book ending on a cliffhanger, keeping the audience reading, just like the TV series keeps the audience watching.

Strategizing the TV Series Transition Into a Book Series

1. Serialized Storytelling: Think of each season as individual books in your series.

2. Character Arcs: The characters we meet in your first book can lead to detailed backstories, personal challenges, and growth arcs that span multiple books. Secondary characters introduced briefly can get their own spotlight in later books.

3. Expanding the Universe: The world introduced in the pilot serves as a nucleus. With each novel, you can expand this story universe – introducing new settings or time periods.

The Profit Plan of a Book Series

Tantalizing readers with an ongoing storyline, relatable characters, and an evolving universe is not merely a creative choice. It's a strategic economic maneuver. The argument that series can be more profitable hinges on several factors.

1. The Snowball Effect: Imagine you've written a phenomenal book. Readers plunge into your world, forge connections with your characters, and then ... it ends. If they're enchanted by Book One, it's highly probable they'll want to read Books Two and Three. One sale can lead seamlessly to multiple sales.

2. Marketing Momentum: Marketing a book is challenging. Yet, when you have a series, each promotional effort you put into one book can have a domino effect on the others. Your marketing efforts compound, as does their impact. The release of each new book creates an opportunity to revitalize interest in the preceding ones, keeping your entire series buoyant in the market.

3. Devoted Readership: As readers spend more time in your story universe, their attachment to your characters and stories grows. Not only does this mean they're likely to purchase subsequent books, but they will become advocates for your work, recommending it to other readers.

4. Multiplying Revenue Streams: Having several books under one thematic umbrella lets you explore various pricing and bundling strategies. Boxed sets or special pricing for purchasing the entire series entice readers to spend more at one time, increasing your revenue.

5. Universe and Spin-off Potential: Once you've built a world and a set of characters, the opportunities to expand on them are abundant. You can create spin-offs, prequels, and side stories all from your story universe, further growing the life span (and the revenue stream) of your series.

The Series Publishing Plan

Have two, or even better, three books, written before you publish your first in a series. This way there is not a years-long gap between books and you can keep your readers interested and buying. If your project is a stand alone (publishing speak for a one off), is there a way it could become a series? Many feature scripts are developed with sequels in mind. Or look at *Fast and Furious*; that was supposed to be a stand alone.

Note: If your script is a stand alone, don't be discouraged. People do read and buy stand-alone books just like they go to stand alone movies.

Take Aways

- Because of read through it is easier to sell and market a series than a stand alone novel.

- Have at least two books written in a series before you publish the first so that you can avoid long stretches between books and keep readers' interest.

Action Steps

1. If your project is a stand-alone, could it be a series?

2. Brainstorm the plots for your next two books.

Part Three: After Writing

You're not finished yet, but the finish line is within sight! It's time to polish your story to perfection with an editor. Then comes all the things you need to publish your book from book blurbs, bios, and covers. It's the final countdown!

Step 11: Hire an Editor

> 👣 Hiring an editor is like having a wise and experienced friend who wants to see you succeed! In this step, I'll discuss the different types of editors, how to find the perfect match for your project, and why investing in professional editing is crucial for your novel's success. Get ready to polish your story until it shines!

So, you think you've finished your book. You've labored over many drafts. Your friends and family say it's brilliant. Your writers group loved it. However, there is one very important step you must take before you are ready to publish: hiring an editor. It is time to get a fresh, objective view of your book.

Do I Really Need an Editor?

Yes. There are two steps that you should spend money on: an editor and a book cover designer (Step 12).

You want to produce a high quality book. Successful authors use editors for feedback and creative support. You need another pair of eyes and an unbiased brain on your story. Editors don't just edit; they enhance, elevate, and strengthen your novel. Their expertise ensures that your words don't just tell a story but resonate, linger, and impact readers.

As a reader, it is easy to tell when writers have skipped this crucial step. In a sea of fiction, making your novel stand out is crucial. This investment is not just financial, but an investment in your author.

What an Editor Will Help You With

Plot Cohesiveness: They dissect plot structures to make sure your story is cohesive and logical. An editor can identify subplots that may divert attention from the main narrative or characters that do not contribute meaningfully to the story. They offer suggestions for refinement or elimination to maintain focus and consistency.

Character Development: They ensure that characters' actions, speech, and evolutions align.

Pacing Perfection: They examine the ebb and flow of action, dialogue, and exposition driving the story forward. They suggest cutting sluggish sections that might lose a reader's interest.

Smooth Transitions: Editors make sure the reader is effortlessly guided from one section to the next. Ensuring that transitions between scenes, chapters, and various elements of the story are smooth and logical is vital.

Maintaining Consistency: Editors ensure that the author's voice remains consistent throughout the narrative, preventing jarring inconsistencies that might distract or confuse readers.

Chapter and Scene Structuring: Effective editors also help ensure that each chapter drives the story forward, ending at points that entice readers to turn the page.

Types of Editors

Hiring a human editor prioritizes quality, reader engagement, and narrative finesse in your book. In the publishing world, there are four different kinds of editors, each with a specialized focus and role. You do not need to invest in all four. I suggest a developmental editor is what new novelists need the most. If you are only going to hire one editor, make it a developmental one.

1. Developmental Editor or a Book/Writing Coach

Focus: Big-Picture Content and Structure

Key Responsibilities:

- **Structural Cohesion:** Developmental editors analyze the overall structure of the story, ensuring that it is coherent and logical.

- **Plot Development:** They assess and provide feedback on the plot, identifying any holes or inconsistencies.

- **Character Development:** They evaluate the authenticity and consistency of character development throughout the story.

- **Pacing and Tension:** Developmental editors examine the narrative arc, ensuring that pacing is tension-filled to keep the reader engaged.

Timing: A developmental editor should be hired early, ideally after the first draft is completed, to provide valuable feedback that will guide subsequent revisions.

2. Line Editor

Focus: Sentence-Level Refinement

Key Responsibilities:

- **Language Enhancement:** Line editors focus on elevating the language, ensuring sentences are not only grammatically correct but also vibrant and varied.

- **Tone and Style:** They ensure that the author's voice remains consistent, and the tone aligns with the genre and target audience.

- **Readability:** Line editors work to enhance the flow and readability of the text, smoothing out awkward constructions and enhancing clarity.

Timing: Engage a line editor after developmental editing to ensure that the language is polished prior to the more detailed mechanical and fact check.

3. Copy Editor

Focus: Language and Formatting Consistency

Key Responsibilities:

- **Grammar and Syntax**: Copy editors dive deeper than proofreaders, ensuring not only mechanical accuracy but also correct grammar, syntax, and usage.
- **Fact-Checking:** They verify dates, events, and factual statements for accuracy.
- **Redundancy and Clarity:**
- They ensure the text is clear, concise, and free of repetition.

Timing: Employ a copy editor after the manuscript has undergone developmental editing and revisions, but before the final proofread.

4. Proofreader

Focus: Mechanical Accuracy

Key Responsibilities:

- **Error Elimination:** Proofreaders meticulously scour your manuscript for typographical, grammatical, punctuation, and formatting errors.

- **Consistency:** They ensure consistency in spelling, hyphenation, numerals, fonts, and capitalization.

- **Formatting:** Proofreaders ensure the manuscript adheres to a consistent format, checking page numbers, headers, footers, and ensuring uniformity in the visual presentation.

Timing: Engage a proofreader after all other editing phases are complete and just before you're ready to publish your manuscript.

While it is still important to have a human (even if it is just a friend) proofread your manuscript before you hit publish, I suggest using a program like ProWritingAid to proofread several times during your writing process. It will catch missing words, double words, grammar mistakes, passive voice, and remind you where to put those pesky commas.

Investing in professional editing is investing in your novel's success and your evolution as an author.

How to Find an Editor

1. **Reedsy.com:** Reedsy offers a curated list of freelance editors with experience in the publishing industry, allowing you to browse profiles and select editors based on their previous work.

2. **Writing Conferences and Workshops:** At writing conferences, workshops, and seminars, you can network with editors and other publishing professionals. Editors may even lead some workshops, giving you a chance to experience their approach and expertise firsthand.

3. **Writing Groups and Forums:** Writing groups and forums, either in your local area or online, are an excellent source for recommendations.

4. **Book Credits:** While reading books (especially those similar to your own), check the acknowledgment section. Authors often thank their editors.

5. **Editorial Freelancers Association** (the-efa.org) matches writers with freelance editors.

A Few Tips on Choosing the Right Editor

1. **Editorial Experience:** Look for an editor with experience in your genre or field.

2. **Sample Edit:** Consider asking for a sample edit of your reader magnet to understand their editing style. You may have to pay for a sample edit, but it is worth the expense to get a sense of how they work.

3. **Previous Work:** Check their portfolio or previously edited books and, if possible, read some of them.

4. **Client Feedback:** Look for reviews or testimonials from previous clients.

5. **Contract Clarity:** Ensure you have clear agreements in writing about the scope of work, timeline, and payment.

Finding an editor who understands and resonates with your work is paramount. Spending time finding the right match is an investment in your book's success and your development as a writer. The best editor for you will not only understand the mechanics of good writing but also connect with your work on a deeper level, ensuring that your voice is preserved and enhanced.

How Much Does an Editor Cost?

Editors and book coaches range in price, depending on their experience. They can charge per word, per page, or a flat fee.

Take Aways

1. Using an editor helps ensure your book is high quality.

2. There are four types of editors: developmental/book & writing coach, line editor, copy editor, proofreader.

3. The most important for beginning novelists is a developmental editor.

4. Use proofreading software like ProWritingAid.

Action Steps

1. Find three developmental editors/book coaches you are interested in working with.

2. Email them to find out their rates and preferred genres.

3. Ask them for a sample edit of your reader magnet.

4. Hire your editor, making sure that you have in writing the agreed on payment, the scope of the work, and the due date.

Step 12: Hire a Cover Designer

> Your book cover is like a beautiful invitation to your story, and we want to make sure it's irresistible! In this step, well explore the importance of a professional book cover, share tips for finding the right designer, and guide you through the process of creating a cover that captures your novel's essence. Get ready to dress your book to impress!

The old adage "don't judge a book by its cover" is dead wrong in publishing. Your cover is the biggest asset you have for marketing. A bad cover on a good book can tank sales and a brilliant cover on a mediocre book can explode sales. It is the movie poster for your book and the number one piece of marketing. Even though most book sales are online now, the cover tells your potential reader what your book is about with one glance.

An impressive cover not only forms the first interaction between your book and potential readers, but also serves as a powerful marketing tool that can dramatically impact your sales and recognition. Your book cover is the first marketing tool that attracts readers, even before they read the blurb or sample the prose.

Since online stores display books as small thumbnails, making sure your cover retains clarity, impact, and recognizability in a small size is paramount.

Genre in Book Covers

Cover design, including images and fonts, is genre specific. You can't use a thriller font on a cozy mystery. It won't attract the right readers and your book won't make money. For example, most thrillers have a picture of a man running away with his back to us. Readers see that image and immediately know the genre. Your cover should instantaneously communicate the genre and tone of the book. This is why way back in Step 1 Read in Your Genre I had you notice cover design.

Ensuring that your cover accurately reflects the genre not only aids in attracting the right audience but also significantly boosts reader satisfaction because they get the story they consciously (or subconsciously) expected.

DIY vs. Professional Design

While it may be tempting to try designing your own cover, I don't recommend it. Without professional expertise, chances are you will end up with a cover that leads to poor or zero sales. Professional cover designers understand all the moving pieces that make a cover brilliant.

Employing a professional designer might seem like a big investment, but it's worth investing in a cover that does justice to your story, adheres to genre norms, and attracts readers. A meticulously crafted cover signals quality.

Branding

As an indie author, the cover is not merely a reflection of your book, but also of you as a brand. Whether you have a series or stand alone books, visual consistency across all your titles makes your books instantly recognizable. This visual identity establishes your author brand. A professional designer can help create a consistent and recognizable aesthetic that becomes synonymous with your name and work. For authors venturing into series, maintaining visual continuity is vital.

Choosing to invest in a professional cover designer is choosing to highlight your writing, presenting your work in the best way.

Where to Find a Cover Designer

Look in some of the same places you look for an editor.

1. Reedsy.com: Reedsy offers a curated list of freelance cover designers with experience in publishing, allowing you to browse profiles and see portfolios.

2. 100covers.com: This service offers quality covers at reasonable prices.

3. Writing Groups and Forums: Joining writing groups and forums, either in your local area or online, is a good source for recommendations.

4. Book Credits: While reading books (especially those similar to your own), check the copyright page or acknowledgments. The cover designer's name and contact info are often listed.

How to Hire a Cover Designer by Sending a Creative Brief

When you hire any kind of artist, it is a smart practice to give them detailed directions in writing a creative brief. A creative brief ensures that you and the artist are both on the same page about the project. Here are some things to include:

1. Reference Images: It is best to pull images from stock photo sites. You do not want your designer inadvertently using copyrighted material. The other option is to use AI image generators like Dall-E and Midjourney. ChatGPT, Microsoft Bing, and Canva use text to generate images, so you don't have to learn how to write prompts. (More about using AI in Step 13 Write Your Book Blurb) Think of these reference images as a mood board for your cover.

2. Your Genre

3. Your Book Blurb: For the dust jacket for hardbacks and the back cover for paperbacks. (Step 13)

4. Your Headshot: These are included on dust jackets and the back cover of paperbacks. (Step 15)

5. Your Bio: These are included on dust jackets and the back cover of paperbacks. (Step14) These are included on dust jackets and the back cover of paperbacks.

6. How Many Revisions: How many times the artist will change the cover from your feedback.

7. The Turnaround Time: How long it will take the artist to complete the work.

8. You Receive the Image Files: (With and without text) so that you have them to use in ads and upload to the online stores.

Take Aways

1. Your cover and your blurb (Step 13) are the two most important pieces of marketing material to sell your book.

2. Think of your cover as your book's movie poster.

3. Your cover must work as a thumbnail.

4. Covers are genre specific.

5. No DIY. Hire a professional.

6. Use a creative brief to hire your cover designer.

Action Steps

1. Pull or generate reference pictures.

2. Write your creative brief.

3. Hire your designer.

Step 13: Write Your Book Blurb

> Your book blurb is like a tantalizing movie trailer that leaves readers eager to dive into your story and click the buy button! In this step, I'll teach you how to craft a compelling blurb that hooks readers, showcases your unique voice, and leaves them wanting more. Get ready to create a killer blurb!

What is a Book Blurb?

A book blurb is a brief and engaging description of a book found on the back cover or online product page. It is not a detailed synopsis. It's a marketing tool that, together with your cover, helps the reader decide to buy your book.

A book blurb is a succinct, magnetic pitch. It's all about intriguing your reader. The blurb must:

- **Spark Curiosity:** Make the reader ask, "What happens next?"

- **Evoke Emotion:** Like excitement, fear, romance, or intrigue.

- **Promise a Journey:** Hint at the adventure the reader will go on.

A great blurb can make the difference between a reader simply browsing and making a purchase.

Here is a fun, easy way to write your book blurb.

The Project Cocktail Pitch:

I call this short pitch a project cocktail pitch because it is how you describe your latest project when someone asks you what you're working on at a cocktail party. Some people call this an elevator pitch, but I think that cocktail pitch is more fun. You can use this approach to pitch screenplays, too.

How to Write a Compelling Book Blurb (the Project Cocktail Pitch)

1. Hook your audience with **an emotional**

hook. Emotion sells. Make your characters' struggle relatable. You can use a metaphor: office politics is high school with suits; an archetype: the high school mean girl is now ruling the PTA. Or ask a question: have you ever wondered what happened to the high school mean girl?

2. Next, introduce **your main character and their emotional drive**. Katniss is an ordinary 16 year-old girl whose selfless sacrifice to save her sister's life starts a revolution.

3. Then, it's onto the **Story Appetizer**, which is three to five sentences about your story. Here is where you can share a bit more about the main character, what they are trying to accomplish, and how they do it. If you need to, here is where you can talk about the world of the story and the bad guy.

4. Finally, end on a **Cliffhanger**. Emphasize the emotional stakes. Can your characters do it? Will she get a date to the wedding or be at the singles table with the great aunts? Will they rob the bank so Joe can get his kidney transplant?

With the cliffhanger, you leave your reader on the edge of their seat. They want to know how the story ends, which translates to a book sale.

Ideally, a blurb should be between 100-150 words. It needs to be concise, focused, and engaging. To help keep your blurb focused, talk about one or two characters at the most.

If your project is in an alternate world, usually fantasy or science fiction, you can start your blurb with the movie trailer phrase "in a world where..." Then connect back with your main character and her emotional drive.

Example: In a world where magic is forbidden, one girl's power could be the key to either salvation or destruction.

Next Write Your Tagline

A tagline is a brief, catchy statement that encapsulates the essence of your book. Think of the sentence on a movie poster. *Live. Die. Repeat* from *Edge of Tomorrow* is one of my favorites. It is easier to write your tagline after your blurb because you have already boiled down your story.

Start with your emotional hook. Is there a way to make it simpler, shorter, and more dramatic? Your tagline becomes the first sentence of your blurb. It hooks the reader to keep reading and get to the hook.

How to Craft a Tagline

1. Be Concise and Memorable: Aim for a short, catchy phrase. Think of it like a movie slogan—something that stays with the reader.

2. Capture the Essence: Your tagline should reflect the core theme or emotional impact of your story.

3. Create Intrigue: Pose a question or present a paradox that piques curiosity.

4. Use Strong, Vivid Language: Choose words that evoke imagery and emotion.

Example: In a game of deceit, trust is a luxury she can't afford.

The Difference Between a Hook and a Tagline

Hooks and taglines are similar, but not the same. A hook is more detailed than a tagline and usually provides some insight into the plot, characters, conflict, or setting of the story.

Characteristics of a Hook:

- **Longer and More Descriptive:** Usually a sentence or two, providing more detail about the story.

- **Story-Focused:** Gives a glimpse into the story's premise, conflict, or characters.

- **Intriguing:** Designed to pique curiosity and pull the reader into wanting to know more.

A tagline, on the other hand, is a very brief phrase or sentence that captures the essence, theme, or tone of the book in a catchy way. It's used in marketing or on the front cover of a book. Taglines are less about the story's details and more about creating an emotional or thematic connection with the reader.

Characteristics of a Tagline:

- **Short and Snappy:** Often just a few words, making it easy to remember.

- **Thematic or Emotional Appeal:** Highlights the underlying theme or emotional journey, rather than specific plot points.

- **Memorable and Catchy:** Designed to stick in the reader's mind.

Imagine a novel about a time-traveling detective:

- **Hook:** A police detective from 1920 leaps through time to solve crimes that haven't happened yet, only to find that changing the past could shatter his future.

- **Tagline:** Time is his beat.

Using Generative AI to Help You With Your Blurbs

From the printing press to the word processor to digital books, writers have always been terrified that technology will ruin writing. Story technology took another leap forward with the introduction of ChatGPT, an artificial intelligence (AI) writing tool.

Now, before you rail against the rise of machines destroying artistic creativity, you are actually already using AI in your daily life. In Word, the predictive text function and the grammar and spelling checks are run by AI. In fact, Microsoft Office, including Word, Excel, PowerPoint, and Teams now includes AI features. The two most popular grammar and punctuation tools, Grammarly and ProWritingAid, are also powered by AI. Recently Bing search, Adobe Illustrator, and Canva have all integrated AI technology. Even my Android phone now has AI to write text messages.

If you are anti-AI, you are going to have a hard time avoiding it.

A lot of writers are terrified because they think AI is going to replace them. Writing AI will not replace writers. Currently, you can't press a button and generate a screenplay or novel. That day may come, but it is not where we are now. And even when it does, computers will never be as creative as human beings.

How you use AI in your creative career is up to you. Some people use it to write their books. Some use it to help them brainstorm and refine ideas or to write marketing plans and ad copy. AI is brilliant at the tasks you may not want to do, like writing taglines, blurbs, and ads.

Generative AI relies on the creativity of the person asking the questions (which are called prompts.) If you don't ask creative questions, you do not get creative answers. It is a tool to level up your creativity and writing. You can use it to brainstorm, analyze, and help you over writers' block.

If you haven't tried AI, play with it. Play is the operative word because it is fun. Brainstorming and storytelling, creating new worlds and characters is a blast! That is why we do it.

How AI Works

What writers call AI are Large Language Models (LLM). LLMs are AI systems capable of understanding and generating human-like text. These models are trained on vast datasets of language, allowing them to grasp nuances in language, context, and even style. Their predictive capabilities enable them to complete sentences, paragraphs, or entire stories based on the instructions they receive. LLMs [do not plagiarize](#) other people's writing. They are outputting original material based on what they have learned about language from everything they have "read."

AI is not evil; people are. Tools can be used for good or bad. A hammer can build a house or hit someone on the head. How you use it is up to you.

How to Use AI to Write Your Book Blurb

Book blurbs are challenging for authors. It is hard to get the gist of your book into just a few words and make it snappy and fun. Lots of authors are using generative AI to help them with their book blurbs. Think of it as your creative assistant, giving you ideas that you edit to make your own.

The two tools I recommend for these tasks are ChatGPT 4o (chatgpt.com) and Claude (claude.ai). As of this writing, ChatGPT 4o is free and Claude is $19.99 a month.

ChatGPT and Claude work the same way, but you get different results. It is fun to ask them the same questions and compare their answers. You can upload your entire book and ask them to analyze it.

To get meaningful results, you will need to write effective prompts, which are the questions and directions that you give the AI. Once you get a result, you can refine the prompt, saying what you like and don't like until you get something you are happy with. The AI remembers what you have told it and learns from every iteration.

Sample Prompts and Hints:

- Always include your genre.
- Always ask it to write a blurb (or ad copy) for a bestselling book.
- Be specific with as much information as possible.

- *Please tell me what the major tropes are in this book. Next, please use some of these tropes to write a book blurb for a bestselling thriller.*

- *Write me a bestselling book burb for this science fiction thriller.*

- Once you have a blurb you like, upload the blurb and ask for 10 taglines based on the blurb. Refine the taglines and pick your favorite.

Take Aways

- A book blurb is a brief and engaging description of a book found on the back cover or online product page. It is not a detailed synopsis.

- It's a marketing tool that, together with your cover, helps the reader decide to buy your book.

- A **tagline** is a brief, catchy statement that encapsulates the essence of your book. Use it for the first sentence of your blurb.

- Use generative AI to help you write your blurb if you're stuck.

    - Make sure your prompts are specific.

    - Always include your genre and bestseller/ing.

The Blurb (Cocktail Pitch) Formula

1. The Emotional Hook

2. Main character and their emotional drive

3. Story Appetizer

4. Cliffhanger

Action Steps

1. Write your blurb.

2. Write your tagline.

3. Practice using AI for blurbs and taglines.

Step 14: Write Your Bio

> Your author bio is like a friendly handshake that introduces you to your readers! In this step, I'll share tips for writing a bio that showcases your personality, establishes your credentials, and helps readers connect with you.

Your bio builds your brand as an author. It's a personal touch that connects you with the reader. Remember, in the indie publishing landscape, you are not just selling a book; you are selling a story and a storyteller.

It's crucial to present not just your story but also yourself effectively. Two key elements in introducing yourself are your author logline and your bio. You need a bio for the back of your book to introduce yourself to readers, your website, and podcast appearances.

Your Writer Logline

The first sentence of your bio is what I call your writer logline. As screenwriters, you are no doubt familiar with loglines. Did you know you need one too?

But before we get to your logline, you need to figure out what kind of stories you write. Write descriptions of all your creative projects: scripts, books, finished and unfinished. Include half-formed ideas. What is the connective tissue of all of these stories? It could be a theme, an emotion, a reoccurring character, or even a favorite trope. This story connection is a key part of your author logline.

The formula is: I write + your genre + kind of books + your personality.

Here are two of my favorite examples:

- Ines Johnson: I write kissing books.

- Jami Albright: I write books that are sexy, swoony, and pee your pants funny.

(While you're at it, I recommend crafting a screenwriting logline as well. It's the same formula. Just add your format - feature - TV drama - TV animation.)

Your Origin Story

Every superhero has an origin story. Peter Parker was bitten by a radioactive spider. Superman escaped Krypton in a rocket and was found in a Kansas cornfield by John and Martha Kent. You have an origin story, too. It's that moment when you discovered your love of storytelling. To discover your origin story, I like to use a technique called **It All Started With** that I learned from the wonderful writing teacher Alexandra Franzen.

You literally say "It all started with" and then in a few sentences tell the story that launched your passion. The next step is to explain how your origin story helped you realize what you wanted to do. Then, round it out with what you are doing now.

So, the formula is:

It all started with _____ and that's when I realized _____ and now I _____.

To show you what I mean, here's mine:

It all started with *Three Days of the Condor*. I was three years old and my dad had taken me to see the spy classic. It was the climax of the film, and the tension was palpable in the audience. Robert Redford was trapped at gunpoint by the villain. In a clear voice I called out, "don't worry, he used to be a bad guy, but now he's good." And that, of course, was exactly what happened next. In that moment, my love of movies and knack for storytelling was born.

Readers love to hear how their favorite authors became writers.

Writing an Engaging Author Bio

1. Start with your author logline.

2. Your origin story in a sentence or two.

3. Add a personal touch. Share a bit about your personal life. Here is where you could mention your screenwriting credits, where you live or grew up.

4. Your favorite things: When I'm not writing you will find me ... binging K dramas and hanging out with my dog.

5. End with a Call to Action: Encourage readers to connect with you by signing up for your newsletter.

Example: Jane crafts thrillers that challenge perceptions with psychological twists. She became interested in what makes good people do bad things when her childhood best friend's dad was arrested for being a con artist. When she's not writing, she enjoys exploring the back roads of America. To find out about her next book, sign up for Jane's newsletter at Jane.com/newsletter.

Take Aways

Bio Formula

1. Your author logline: I write + your genre + kind of books + your personality.

2. Your origin story: It all started with _____ and that's when I realized _____ and now I _____.

3. A personal touch

4. Your favorite things

5. End with a call to action to sign up for your newsletter.

Action Steps

1. Write your bio

Step 15: Get a Headshot

> 👣 Say cheese! Your author headshot is like a warm smile that greets your readers and makes them feel welcome in the world you have created! In this step, we'll discuss the importance of a professional headshot and share tips for capturing your best self. Get ready to put your best face forward!

You will need a headshot to accompany your bio. Don't worry if you don't have the budget for a professional photo shoot. You don't need anything fancy, just a picture that is in focus and attractive with good lighting. Have a friend take your picture against a plain background. Don't forget to smile!

Take Aways

1. A headshot lets your readers see the real you.

2. A headshot is an important compliment to your bio.

Action Steps

1. Take some pictures.

2. Pick your favorite to use as your headshot with your bio.

Step 16: Write Your Back Matter

> 👣 Your book's back matter is like a bonus feature that keeps readers engaged even after they've finished your story! In this step, we'll explore the various elements you can include in your back matter, from author notes to sneak peeks of your next project. We'll talk about how to use this space to engage readers, provide extra content, and promote your next book. Get ready to create back matter that leaves readers wanting more! Let's turn those final pages into a treasure trove of value!

Turning a screenplay into a novel involves more than just adapting your story; it encompasses the entire process of book creation, right down to the details like back matter.

What is Back Matter?

Back matter is the material found at the end of a book, after the story. It's not filler; it's a strategic space that can be used for marketing and reader engagement. Unlike front matter (which includes things like the title page and table of contents), readers read back matter after they have finished and enjoyed your book, making it a prime spot for connecting deeper with them.

The Importance of Back Matter

Effective back matter keeps readers engaged with your work even after they've finished the book by giving a sneak peek of the first few chapters of the next book, a link to buy the next book, and offering your reader magnet and newsletter sign up. Back matter is an important part of marketing, building fans, and getting readers to buy your next book.

Kinds of Back Matter

The content of back matter can vary, but here are some common and effective elements:

1. Preview/Buy Link of Next Book: Include a teaser or an excerpt from your next book that ends in a buy link to encourage purchases. Many authors include the first chapter of the next book here.

2. List of Other Works: If you have other published works, list them here with a link to your website to encourage purchases.

3. About the Author: Your bio

4. Call to Action: Encourage readers to leave a review on Amazon and sign up for your newsletter.

5. Acknowledgments: This section is to thank those who helped in the creation of your book, from editors to supportive family members.

6. Author's Note: This can be a space for sharing the inspiration behind your novel. Maybe it was based on a true story or inspired by something in your life. Here is a good place to mention your story started as a screenplay.

7. Discussion Questions for Book Clubs: It is also a good practice to include book club discussion questions on your website.

Writing Effective Back Matter

- **Keep it relevant and engaging:** Make sure that whatever you include in your back matter is relevant to your readers and adds value to the book.

- **Maintain your voice:** The back matter should reflect your unique voice and style as an author.

- **Encourage interaction:** Use this space to encourage readers to engage with you further by signing up for your newsletter and buying more books.

Every element of your book offers an opportunity to connect with readers and build your brand. Back matter is more than just the final pages of your book; it's a powerful tool that can enhance reader engagement, offer additional value, and promote your work.

Take Aways

1. Back matter is the material in the back of the book after the story.

2. Back matter is prime real estate to sell your next book, give away your lead magnet, get sign ups to your newsletter, and ask for Amazon reviews.

Action Steps

1. Write your call to action to get newsletter subscribers. Add it to the end of your bio.

2. Write your acknowledgments.

3. Write your author's note.

4. Write your book club discussion questions. (Hint: You can ask Claude or ChatGPT to suggest questions.)

Step 17: Format Your Book

> Formatting your book is like giving it a makeover! In this step, I'll guide you through the process, share tips for creating a visually appealing layout, and help you make your book look its best on every device, making each page visually appealing and a joy to read. Get ready to make your book look as good on the inside as it does on the outside!

Book formatting is the process of structuring and designing a book's interior to ensure it is aesthetically pleasing and readable. As an indie author, you will format your book for hardbacks, paperbacks, and e-books.

Why is Book Formatting Important?

1. Professional Appearance: Properly formatted books look professional, enhancing credibility and reader trust.

2. Readability: Good formatting improves readability, making the reading experience enjoyable.

3. Genre Expectations: Different genres have different formatting standards. Meeting these expectations improves reader experience and satisfaction.

4. Platform Requirements: E-book platforms have specific formatting requirements to upload and sell your book.

The formatting tools discussed below have options to help you choose the right fonts and designs for your genre.

Basic Steps in Book Formatting

1. Choose the Right Layout: Decide on your book's size and layout, considering factors like genre and where you will be publishing (print, ebook, or both).

2. Set Margins and Spacing: Margins should be set to ensure comfortable reading, and spacing needs to be consistent throughout.

3. Select Fonts and Headers: Choose readable fonts and design headers and footers (page numbers, book title, author name).

4. Chapter Breaks and Titles: Clearly define chapter breaks and format chapter titles for easy navigation.

5. Front and Back Matter: Include necessary front and back matter like title pages, contents, acknowledgments, and bios. Most of these formatting tools autogenerate a table of contents.

6. Check Platform Specifications: Each publishing platform may have specific formatting requirements, especially for ebooks.

Formatting Tools for Indie Authors

There are several book formatting tools you can use, ranging from paid to free. All the choices do much of the hard work for you by automatically laying out your book in the margins for the format you are designing. Most helpfully, they walk you through all the choices you need to make.

Here is a breakdown of the top tools available, from most expensive to free.

Vellum

- **Overview:** This was the first and is still the most popular book formatting tool among authors. Vellum is known for its ease of use and beautiful, professional layouts.

- **Features:** Offers various templates, easy customization, and the ability to preview how the book will look on different devices. It will autogenerate the different versions you need for each online store.

- **Best For:** Authors seeking an intuitive and visually appealing design process.

- **Con:** Only works on Mac. It is more expensive than the other paid choice, Atticus.

- **Price:** One time purchase of $199.99 for e-books & $249.99 for both e- and print books. I recommend downloading the free version and experimenting with it before you purchase.

Atticus

- **Overview:** Atticus is a newer software compatible with both Windows and Mac. It's gaining popularity for its versatility and user-friendliness. They are adding functions monthly, including word processing, similar to Scrivener.

- **Features:** Provides customizable templates, export options for various platforms, and allows for collaborative work. It has more features and is easier to use than Vellum.

- **Best For:** Authors looking for a cross-platform, comprehensive formatting tool.

- **Price:** $147

Draft2Digital (D2D)

- **Overview:** Known primarily for its publishing distribution service, Draft2Digital also offers a free formatting tool.

- **Features:** Easy to use with basic genre customization options. It converts manuscripts into e-book and print-ready formats.

- **Best For:** Authors who want a simple, no-cost formatting solution.
- **Con:** Limited format options and no customization.
- **Price:** Free

Reedsy

- **Overview:** Reedsy offers a free online book formatting tool.
- **Features:** It has a user-friendly interface with professional templates suitable for both e-books and print.
- **Best For:** Authors seeking a free, simple, cloud-based tool with professional design options.
- **Con:** Limited format options and customization.
- **Price:** Free

Effective book formatting is a critical step in indie publishing, directly affecting the presentation and reception of your novel. While it might seem daunting, especially for those new to the process, the tools available today make it easy to do it yourself.

By selecting the right software and paying attention to the details of formatting, you can ensure your novel looks professional. The quality of your book's formatting is as important as the quality of your writing.

Take Aways

1. Book formatting is designing the interior layout of your book, how the print looks on the page.

2. Book formatting includes choices of font, margins, and chapter design.

3. It is genre specific.

4. There are paid and free software options to format your book.

Action Steps

1. Experiment with the different tools to decide which one you want to use.

2. Format your book. Don't rush this step. Spend time trying different things to decide what you like.

3. Proofread carefully each formatted copy to make sure there were no software hiccups.

Part Four: Publish Your Book

Touchdown! It's time to push the publish button and get your book out into the world. I'll walk you step by step through publishing your e-book and physical book.

All About Indie Publishing

> Self-publishing is not the stigma it once was. It is big business. Authors who publish their own books prefer to call it indie publishing. In the last 15 years, with the debut of the Kindle, indie publishing has exploded. In fact, it is now as big as one of the big five publishers.

With just a few steps, authors can publish their own books. Ebooks can be published with a click of a button. Unlike the past, as an indie author, you don't have to pay vast sums of money to have your physical book published. There are print-on-demand services that authors use to get their books into bookstores and libraries. When they have an event, they can order a bunch of books to sign and sell.

The biggest pro for going indie versus traditional is that an author has control over her copyright. This means she is the owner of her own intellectual property (IP) and can make money off it, however she chooses. Indie authors can sell their books a multitude of ways, earn multiple streams of income, and get them into more readers' hands.

Where to Sell Your Book

While Amazon is the biggest seller of digital books, there are many places authors can sell their e-books:

- Amazon
- Barnes & Noble Press (formerly Nook)
- Kobo (Their biggest market is Canada, although they have users worldwide. Their e-readers sell at Walmart in the United States.)
- Apple books
- Google books
- On your own website

Print books are still a booming business. As an indie author, you can use a variety of print on demand services to sell your books as hardbacks, paperbacks, and even large print.

Where to sell your print book:

- All major online bookstores, including Amazon, Barnes & Noble, and Bookshop.org.
- Brick and mortar bookstores
- Libraries
- In person events like conventions, conferences, and book signings
- On your own website

Audio Books

Audio books are a growing market. Fewer than a third of books have an audio version, but there is a huge audience that prefers to listen to books. Audio books used to be prohibitively expensive to produce, but new tools and technology make them within reach for indie authors.

Where to sell your audio book:

- There are services like Findaway Voices that will distribute your audio book. Findaway is owned by Spotify, which now offers audio books.

- New artificial intelligence (AI) tools make it easy and cost-effective to produce an audio book or you can narrate it yourself.
- You can sell on your own website.

Going Wide

Going wide means you're not putting all your eggs in one basket (which is usually Amazon). Instead, you're spreading your books across many platforms and retailers. This strategy is all about accessibility; making your book available to readers no matter where they prefer to shop, from major e-book retailers to smaller digital outlets, physical bookstores, and even libraries. Most readers have a favorite place to get their books, which is why being everywhere is a smart strategy.

By opting to publish wide, you're exploring the vast ecosystem of digital and physical book sales, including libraries. Did you know that authors make money every time their digital book is checked out? Being in a variety of places significantly boosts your book's visibility, tapping into diverse reader communities and opening up additional revenue streams.

Going wide requires a bit more work and strategy. You'll need to manage your distribution on multiple platforms, keep track of sales and marketing efforts across these channels, and possibly deal with different formatting requirements. Yet, the potential rewards—reaching a wider audience, increasing your income, and gaining more control over where and how your book is sold—are well worth the effort.

Think of publishing wide as an investment in your book's future and your career as an author. It's about tapping into multiple streams of income that can significantly boost your writing career.

Step 18: Get an ISBN

> Getting an ISBN is like giving your book its very own passport to travel the world! In this step, I'll explain what an ISBN is and why it's important and guide you through the process of obtaining one for your novel. Get it to make your book official!

Have you ever wondered about that funky little number on the back of your book? That's the ISBN, which stands for International Standard Book Number. Think of it as the Social Security number for your book. It's a unique identifier that helps the copyright office, booksellers, libraries, and readers find your book among the millions out there. You can't use the same ISBN for digital and print books because they are considered different editions. It's required to sell your book in stores or online.

How to Get Your ISBN

1. Identify Your ISBN Agency

Different countries have different agencies for issuing ISBNs. In the United States, Bowker's MyIdentifiers.com is your go-to. For other countries, check the International ISBN Agency's website for the right contact.

2. Purchase Your ISBN

Head over to your country's ISBN agency website and fill out the application. It's pretty straightforward, like signing up for an online service.

3. Wait for It

After you apply and pay, you'll get your ISBN. The waiting period can vary, so be patient.

How Much Does an ISBN Cost?

The cost can vary by country and the number of ISBNs you buy. Buying in bulk often saves money in the long run. As of this writing, in the U.S.: A single ISBN costs $125, but if you're planning to publish multiple books, you can get a batch of 10 for $295, 100 for $575, or even 1,000 for $1,500. Prices can vary, so check the latest on Bowker's website. Also, you need an ISBN for each edition of your book (e-book, hardback, paperback) so I suggest buying 10 for $295.

Elsewhere: Costs can vary widely. In some countries, ISBNs are free, while in others, they might cost a bit. The key is to check with your local ISBN agency.

Getting an ISBN is a big step in your publishing journey. It might seem bureaucratic, but it's actually a milestone that brings your book closer to readers around the world.

In the U.S., go to MyIdentifiers.com, set up an account, and decide how many you need. It's a straightforward process: buy, assign, and register your ISBN to your book.

Take Aways

1. You need an ISBN to get copyright and sell books.

2. An ISBN is like your book's Social Security number.

3. You need an ISBN for each format of your book (hardback, paperback, e-book, audio) so, you may consider buying in bulk.

Action Steps

1. Decide how many formats you are publishing.

2. Go to MyIdentifiers.com and set up an account.

3. Purchase your ISBNs.

Step 19: Get Your Copyright

> 👣 Getting your copyright is like giving your story a protective shield! In this step, we'll discuss the importance of copyright, explain how to register your work, and share tips for protecting your intellectual property. Get ready to safeguard your creative masterpiece!

An author needs a copyright to protect their original work from being copied or used without their permission. It also allows you to make money from your work by selling or licensing it.

To get a copyright, you apply online with the Copyright Office. The website looks like it hasn't been updated since 1995; it is unwieldy with lots of steps. Apparently, it is optimized for the Firefox web browser, so if you have any trouble, use that. I have always used Chrome, and it's been fine. The application can be confusing, so I will walk you through it step by step.

To Get a Copyright You Will Need:

- A Manuscript to Upload
- An ISBN
- A credit card for the $65 payment

The first time you copyright something, you will have to make an account.

How to Apply for a Copyright

1. Go to copyright.gov/registration
2. Click the blue box, which says "Log into the Copyright Office Electronic Registration System."
3. Next Screen: On the left-hand side there is a login box. Click Create Your Account and then log in.

4. On the left, under Register a Work, click on the blue standard work.

5. On the next screen, on the left, is a list of the screens you will fill in. Hit continue on the right to move from screen to screen. If you need to go back, click the category on the list on the left that you want to return to.

6. Type of work: Literary work

7. Titles: The title of your book

8. Publication: The date you published your book. It can be today's date.

9. Authors: Your name or your pen name

10. Claimants: Your name. The claimant owns the copyright.

11. Limitations of Claim: Skip

12. Rights & Permissions: You agree you own the rights and permissions to the work.

13. Correspondent: You. This is who people will contact if they want to get permission to use your work.

14. Mail Certificate: The address where the copyright office will mail the copyright cer-

tificate.

15. Special Handling: This is an extra payment to expedite processing. You don't need this. Your work is covered the minute you register it.

16. Certification: You sign your application electronically.

17. Review Submission: Check that your information is correct.

18. Pay: This seems counterintuitive; you have to pay before you upload your book.

19. Upload your Manuscript

It can take up to eight weeks for you to receive your certificate from the copyright office. Don't worry; your work is legally protected the minute you register it.

Take Aways

1. An author needs a copyright to protect their original work from being copied or used without their permission.

2. Copyright lasts for the life of the author plus 70 years after her death (in the United States.)

3. Apply online with the Copyright Office to get your copyright.

4. To get your copyright you will need:

- A Manuscript to Upload

- An ISBN

- A credit card for the $65 payment

Action Steps

1. Get your copyright online.

Step 20: Upload Your E-book to Retailers

> 👣 It's time to take your book global! I'll guide you through the process of uploading your e-book to various retailers, making sure your story reaches as many readers as possible. Let's get your book on every digital shelf out there!

Amazon is the biggest bookstore in the world, so publishing your e-book there is a huge part of your publishing plan. But there are other digital book retailers. Readers have their preferred platforms and often only buy from one place. You are missing substantial sales if you only use Amazon. Here is a breakdown of all the places you should list your book and how to do it.

Publishing Your Ebook on Amazon

Kindle Direct Publishing (KDP) is Amazon's self-publishing service that allows authors to publish their books directly to Kindle and Amazon.

Uploading Your E-book to KDP

1. Create a KDP Account: at kdp.amazon.com.

2. Add a New Kindle E-Book: Click on "+ Kindle e-book" in your KDP dashboard.

3. Enter Book Details: Add your book title, blurb, bio and headshot, keywords, and categories. These details help readers find your book on Amazon.

4. Upload Your Manuscript: Upload your manuscript as an ePub.

5. Upload Your Cover

6. Set Rights and Pricing: Choose all the territories where you want to sell your book (everywhere) and set your price.

Pricing and Amazon's Revenue Share

E-books: For e-books priced between $2.99 and $ 9.99, Amazon currently pays 70% in royalties, keeping a 30% commission. Outside this range, the royalty rate is 35%.

Kindle Unlimited

Kindle Unlimited is a subscription service that lets subscribers read as many books as they like from an extensive selection for a monthly fee. It includes a wide range of genres and titles, both from traditional publishers and self-published authors.

How Kindle Unlimited Works for Authors

- **KDP Select Enrollment:** To have your e-book available on Kindle Unlimited, you must enroll it in KDP Select. This is Amazon's program that offers special perks for authors.

- **Exclusivity Requirement:** Enrolling in KDP Select requires that your e-book be exclusive to Amazon. This means it cannot be sold, published, or distributed on any other digital platform or store, including your own website or libraries.

- **Royalties Based on Pages Read:** Instead of a traditional sale royalty, authors earn money based on the number of pages of their book that are read by Kindle Unlimited subscribers.

- **Monthly Reports:** Authors can track their earnings through monthly reports on their KDP dashboard.

Wide vs. Exclusive

The philosophy of this book is getting multiple streams of income from your idea. That means having as many versions of your book for sale in as many places as possible. This strategy protects you if something goes wrong with your Amazon KDP account. There are horror stories of Amazon taking books offline and authors taking months to get it straightened out. And recently, they lowered the payment per page for Kindle Unlimited.

All that being said, Kindle Unlimited might be the right choice for you. On your indie publishing journey, there are lots of choices. There is no right answer. You must weigh the pros and cons and decide what makes sense for you. Even if you decide to publish your e-books on Kindle Unlimited, you can still be wide with your print books.

Take Aways

1. Kindle Direct Publishing (KDP) is Amazon's self-publishing service that allows authors to publish their books directly to Kindle and Amazon.

2. Amazon has an exclusive subscription service for e-books called Kindle Unlimited.

3. If you participate in Kindle Unlimited, your print books can still be wide.

Action Steps

1. Set up your KDP Account at kdp.amazon.com.

2. Upload your ePub and cover to KDP.

3. Choose all the territories so your book will be on sale everywhere.

Publishing Your E-book on Kobo

Kobo is a Canadian company that sells e-books, audiobooks, and e-readers. Walmart sells Kobo e-readers in the United States. Kobo's global reach provides authors with access to readers in over 190 countries, an easy way to reach an international audience. Kobo is author friendly with great customer service and promotional tools.

Kobo offers a self-publishing platform called **Kobo Writing Life**, which allows authors to easily upload and manage their e-books.

Step-by-Step Guide to Publishing on Kobo

1. Create a Kobo Writing Life Account: at kobo.com/us/en/p/writinglife

2. Start a New E-Book Project: Once logged in, click on Create New e-book.

3. Enter Your E-Book Details: Input your book title, author name, blurb, bio and headshot, categories, and keywords.

4. Upload Your Manuscript: In ePub format.

5. Upload Your Cover

6. Set Geographic Rights: Choose all the countries so readers all over the world can purchase your book.

7. Price Your E-Book: Kobo allows you to set different prices for different countries.

Pricing & Kobo's Revenue Share

- **Setting the Price:** Kobo does not set restrictions on pricing.

- **Revenue Share:** Kobo currently offers a 70% royalty on the list price for books priced above $2.99. For books priced below this threshold, the royalty rate is 45%.

Kobo's Subscription Service - Kobo Plus

Kobo Plus is a subscription service offered by Kobo. It allows readers to access a vast library of e-books for a monthly fee. Here's what you need to know as an author:

- **Opting-In:** When you publish your book on Kobo Writing Life, you can choose to make your book available through Kobo Plus.

- **Royalties in Kobo Plus:** Payments are based on the number of minutes read in your book by subscribers. The more your book is read, the more you earn.

- **Market Reach:** Kobo Plus is popular with its customers.

- **Kobo Plus is non-exclusive:** You can publish your digital books on other platforms.

- **Kobo Plus is another revenue stream for authors.**

Take Aways

1. Kobo is a popular platform in other countries, giving your books a global reach.

2. Author centric customer service.

3. Their subscription service, Kobo Plus, is non-exclusive.

Action Steps

1. Set up your Kobo Writing Life account at kobo.com/us/en/p/writinglife.

2. Upload your manuscript and cover.

3. Opt-in to Kobo Plus.

Publishing your E-book on Barnes & Noble Press

Barnes & Noble Press (formerly Nook) is the self-publishing arm of Barnes & Noble. It allows authors to upload their works and make them available on the Nook bookstore for people reading on the Nook e-reader. It is like Amazon KDP for Kindle books.

Uploading Your E-Book to Barnes & Noble Press

1. Create a Barnes & Noble Press Account: at press.barnesandnoble.com

2. Start a New Project: Click on the Create a New Project button and select E-Book.

3. Enter Book Details: Fill in the title, description, blurb, bio, headshot, keywords, and categories. This information helps readers find your book in the Nook store.

4. Upload Your Manuscript: Upload your novel in ePub format.

5. Upload Your Cover

6. Preview Your E-Book: Use the Nook Press previewer to ensure your book looks as you intended.

7. Set Rights and Distribution: Choose all the territories. Be everywhere.

8. Price Your E-Book: Set the retail price for your e-book.

Pricing Your Book and Barnes & Noble's Revenue

- For e-books priced at $2.99 or above, Barnes & Noble Press currently pays a 65% royalty.
- For e-books priced below $2.99, the royalty rate is 40%.

Take Aways

1. Barnes & Noble Press offers higher royalties if you upload directly instead of using another service.

Action Steps

1. Set up your Barnes & Noble Press account at press.barnesandnoble.com.

2. Upload your ePub file to Barnes & Noble Press.

Apple Books

Apple Books provides a seamless reading experience for Apple device users. It's known for its user-friendly interface and extensive reach, given the vast number of Apple device users globally. Publishing on this platform can significantly increase your book's visibility, reaching a wide audience of Apple users.

Publishing Your E-Book on Apple Books

1. Sign Up for iTunes Connect: Apple Books uses iTunes Connect for its publishing platform. You'll need to create an Apple ID if you don't already have one, and then sign up for iTunes Connect at itunesconnect.apple.com

2. Enroll in the Apple Books for Authors Program: This program allows you to publish your e-books directly to the Apple Books Store.

3. Access the Book Section in iTunes Connect: Once logged in, navigate to the Books section.

4. Provide Book Details: Enter the book title, author name, blurb, bio, headshot, and keywords. This metadata is crucial for making your book discoverable on the platform.

5. Upload Your E-Book and Cover: Upload your ePub file and cover image. Apple also gives the option to add a sample for readers.

6. Set Your Book's Price: Apple Books allows for global pricing, so you can set different prices for different regions.

7. Submit for Review: Once you've uploaded your book and set the price, submit it for review. Apple will review the submission to ensure it meets their guidelines.

8. Book Goes Live: After approval, your book will be available on the Apple Books Store.

Pricing Your Book and Apple's Revenue

- **Apple's Revenue Share:** Currently, Apple

takes a 30% cut of your e-book sales, leaving you with a 70% royalty.

Take Aways

1. Apple has a devoted fan base who prefer to consume content on Apple devices. Don't miss these customers by skipping Apple Books.

Action Steps

1. Set up your iTunes Connect account at itunesconnect.apple.com.

2. Upload your ePub and cover on iTunes Connect.

Google Books

Google Books serves as both a digital bookstore and an extensive book database. It allows users to search the content of books and, if available, purchase or borrow them. As an author, listing your book on Google Books can enhance its discoverability in searches and broaden your audience reach.

Publishing Your E-Book on Google Books

1. Create a Google Play Books Account: To publish on Google Books, you need to sign up for a Google Play Books Partner Account. Go to the Google Play Books Partners Center at play.google.com/books/publish and create an account.

2. Add a New Book: Go to the Book Catalog and select Add Book.

3. Enter Book Details: Provide your book's information, including title, author, blurb, bio, headshot, categories, keywords, and ISBN. This metadata is crucial for discoverability.

4. Upload Your E-Book and Cover Image: Upload your ePub manuscript file and cover art. Google Books also lets you add a preview of your book.

5. Set Your Book's Price: Google Books provides the option to set different prices for different countries.

6. Choose Distribution Settings: Select where and how you want your book to be available. Choose to make it available globally.

7. Publish Your eBook: Submit your book for publishing. Google will review it, and once approved, it will appear on Google Books and the Google Play Store.

Google's Revenue

Google's Revenue Share: Currently, Google takes a 30% commission on e-book sales, which means you receive a 70% royalty.

Take Aways

1. Set up your Google Play Books Partners account at the Google Play Books Partners Center at play.google.com/books/publish.

2. Upload your ePub and cover.

Action Steps

1. Set up your Google Play Books Partners account at the Google Play Books Partners Center at play.google.com/books/publish.

2. Upload your ePub and cover.

Understanding Draft2Digital

Are you completely overwhelmed by all of these retailers? And the accounts you have to create and keep track of? Well, good news! There is a service that will do it all for you!

Draft2Digital (D2D) is a digital self-publishing platform that simplifies the distribution of e-books and print books. D2D offers a streamlined approach to self-publishing, allowing authors to distribute their books to a wide range of retailers and libraries with one upload. They handle the conversion of your manuscript into various e-book formats and provide distribution to major online retailers like Amazon, Apple Books, Barnes & Noble, Kobo, and library systems. D2D is the easiest way to get into the apps that libraries use for digital books. And it will upload your book to Ingram Spark to get the print book in online and brick-and-mortar stores.

Draft2Digital's Services

- **E-book and Print on Demand Distribution:** D2D distributes both e-books and print- on-demand books through Ingram Spark.

- **Universal Book Links (UBLs):** This free

feature at books2read.com generates a single link for your book that directs readers to their preferred retailer. It simplifies sharing your book across different stores.

- **Formatting Tool:** D2D provides a free formatting tool for your manuscript for e-book and print, ensuring it meets various retailers' specifications.

- **Great Customer Service:** Their motto is run by authors for authors.

How Much Does Draft2Digital Cost?

- **No Upfront Costs:** There are no fees currently for uploading or distributing your book via D2D.

- **Royalties:** D2D takes a 10% cut of the retail price.

Warning: D2D's 10% cut is on top of the 30% to 45% that the retailers take. You are paying for D2D doing all the uploading and managing of the retailers. You have to decide which is more important to you: spending more time uploading your book different places and making more money or spending very little time managing the platforms and making less. It is okay to try different tactics. I put my first book out using D2D and this book out uploading individually. Always use D2D to get into the library apps.

Publishing Your Book on Draft2Digital

1. Create a Draft2Digital Account: Sign up for a free account on the Draft2Digital website at pitchmaster.com/draft2digital (affiliate link).

2. Add a New Book: In your dashboard, select the option to add a new book.

3. Upload Your Manuscript: Provide your novel in a standard word processing format like .docx. D2D will convert this into various e-book formats.

4. Enter Book Details: Fill in your book's metadata, including title, author name, blurb, and keywords.

5. Enter your bio and upload your headshot.

6. Upload Your Cover

7. Use the Formatting Tool: If needed, use D2D's formatting tool to ensure your book meets the formatting standards for both e-books and print. Don't forget to proofread the formatting to make sure it looks good.

8. Set Distribution Channels: Choose which retailers and libraries you want your book distributed to.

9. Price Your Book: Determine your book's selling price. D2D provides recommendations but gives you complete control over pricing.

9. Review and Publish: Finalize your choices and submit your book for publishing. D2D will distribute it to the selected channels.

Take Aways

1. If you don't want to manage uploading to all the stores, D2D will do it for you.

2. They charge a flat fee of 10% for every book sold.

3. Their other services are free.

4. Even if you are managing all the retailers, still use D2D to publish to the library apps.

Action Steps

1. Create a D2D account at pitchmaster.com/draft2digital (affiliate link).

2. Upload your book and cover. Format it.

3. Choose the retailers you want to distribute to. Include the library apps.

Step 21: Upload Your Book to Print on Demand Services

> 👣 Uploading your book to print-on-demand services gives your story a tangible form that readers can hold in their hands! In this step, I'll explore the different POD options available, guide you through the uploading process, and share tips to ensure that your

> physical book looks and feels amazing. Get ready to bring your novel to life!

Print on Demand (POD) is a publishing model where books are printed as they are ordered and shipped, rather than in bulk. This approach has revolutionized self-publishing by minimizing upfront costs, reducing risk, and allowing for greater flexibility in book production.

You can use print on demand to sell physical books:

- On online retailers like Amazon, Barnes & Noble, and Bookshop.org.
- At brick-and-mortar stores like your local bookshop.
- On your own website.
- To libraries.
- At live events like conventions, conferences, and book signings.

Key Advantages of Print on Demand:

- **No Large Upfront Costs:** Authors do not

have to pay for large print runs of books.

- **Flexibility:** Offers the ability to easily update the book. If you find a typo, you can fix it immediately.

- **Eco-Friendly:** Less waste since books are printed only when they are bought.

Different Kinds of Print Editions:

- Hardback
- Paperback (Libraries don't buy paperbacks.)
- Large Print
- Special Editions with fancy binding and illustrations

How to Price Your Print on Demand Book

1. Understand Printing Costs: Your book's printing cost is the first factor in setting the retail price. All the services provide a calculator on their website where you can input your book's specifications (like page count, paper type, and dimensions) to find out the cost per copy.

2. Consider Your Profit Margin: After knowing the printing cost, decide on your profit margin. This is the amount you'll earn per book sold. Remember, **retail price = printing cost + the retail cut + your profit.**

3. Factor in Retailers Discounts: Retailers like Amazon or Barnes & Noble expect a discount, typically around 55%. This means if your book retails for $20, the store buys it for $9 (55% off), and you earn the difference minus the printing cost.

What is a Proof Copy?

A proof copy is a copy of your print book that you order before publishing. This way you can proofread one more time and check how it looks. This is a step you do not want to skip!

Top Print-on-Demand Services

Here is a quick overview of the top five print-on-demand services:

- Ingram Spark
- Amazon KDP Print
- Barnes & Noble Press

- Lulu
- Book Vault

Warning: Do not opt for publishing services that require big upfront fees. These are shady companies that take advantage of new authors. The whole point of print-on-demand is you don't have to pay for large print runs.

Why Use Multiple POD Services?

There are strategic benefits to using multiple POD services to maximize your book's reach and potential. Each service has its strengths and combining them can maximize your book's availability and visibility.

- **Wider Distribution:** Different services can distribute your book to bookstores, libraries, and online retailers.

- **Different Product Options:** Some POD services offer unique print options or formats like hardcover editions or special paper types.

- **Backup Plan:** If there's ever an issue with Amazon, having your book available through other channels ensures continuous availability.

Ingram Spark

Ingram Spark is a self-publishing platform that offers independent authors and publishers the opportunity to print, publish, and distribute their books worldwide. It has a vast distribution network to stores and libraries, making it a requirement for indie authors who want to sell print books.

Ingram Spark is the primary catalog that bookstores, libraries, and universities use to order books. These places do not order from Amazon. Listing on Ingram Spark is the way to get your book into your local bookstore and library. Books published through Ingram Spark can be in online stores like Amazon and Barnes & Noble, as well as in thousands of bookstores worldwide. You can also order books for events like in person signings directly from Ingram. If you don't want to upload your book to individual retailers for print to individual retailers, Draft2Digital will upload your book to Ingram Spark for wide distribution.

How to Upload Your Book to Ingram Spark

1. Create an Account: Visit the Ingram Spark website at ingramspark.com and create an account. You'll need to provide some basic information about yourself and your publishing goals.

2. Title Setup: Once your account is created, go to the dashboard and select Add New Title. Fill in the details about your book, including title, author name, book blurb, bio, headshot, and format (paperback or hardback).

3. Upload Your Manuscript: Upload the interior file of your book in PDF format.

4. Upload Your Cover

5. Review and Approve: After uploading, you'll be able to review digital proofs of your book. Carefully check for any errors in formatting or cover alignment.

6. Set Distribution Channels: Choose where you want your book to be available. Ingram Spark offers a wide range of options, including major online retailers like Barnes & Noble and Bookshop.org, brick-and-mortar bookstores, and libraries.

7. Choose Return or Non-Returnable. (I recommend non-returnable. See below.)

8. Set Your Retail Price: Decide on the retail price for your book. Ingram Spark will display the printing costs, which can help you set a competitive and profitable price.

9. Order your Proof

10. Payment and Approval: Pay the title setup fee. Once the payment is processed, Ingram Spark will review your book. This can take a few days.

11. Publish: After approval, your book will be listed as available for distribution. Ingram Spark will print and ship copies as orders come in from retailers.

What Are Returns in Publishing?

In the book industry, 'returns' refer to a policy where retailers can return unsold books to the publisher. There are two types of return policies you can set on Ingram Spark:

1. Returnable: Allows retailers to return unsold books. This is a traditional model in book retailing. If you choose this option, be aware that you will be responsible for the cost of the returned books, which can be significant. I don't recommend returns for indie authors because of the expense. There are further options within this category:

- **Return and Destroy:** The retailer can destroy the unsold books and you pay for the printing cost. No physical books are returned to you.

- **Return and Deliver:** Unsold books are returned to you, and you pay for both the printing and the shipping costs.

2. Non-Returnable: Retailers cannot return unsold books. This option is less risky financially, because you won't incur costs for unsold inventory. However, some bookstores and libraries might be less likely to stock your book if it's non-returnable.

Amazon KDP Print

Besides e-books for the Kindle, Amazon offers its own print-on-demand for paperbacks. This service is only for their store. Luckily, Amazon doesn't demand exclusivity for print books, so you're free to use other POD services too.

For print books, Amazon takes a percentage for printing costs, which varies based on the book's specifications. The remaining revenue after printing cost is split, with the author receiving 60% and Amazon keeping 40%.

Warning: When you use other POD services with Amazon instead of KDP Print, your book can take longer to show up on the site. Consider this timing issue if you are doing a book launch where you want the book available everywhere at the same time.

Uploading Your Book to Amazon KDP Print

1. Amazon KDP (Kindle Direct Publishing): First up, you'll be working with Amazon KDP Print to get your book printed on demand. If you haven't already, create a KDP account.

2. Make Your Manuscript a PDF: Amazon provides detailed guidelines and templates to make this as painless as possible.

3. Make Your Cover a PDF: Amazon requires your cover to be a single PDF, including the back cover, spine, and front cover. Your cover designer should provide this file. The dimensions depend on your book's page count, so use Amazon's calculator to get this right.

4. Create New Title: Go to your KDP dashboard, select Create a New Title, and then choose Paperback. You'll be prompted to enter details like your book's title, blurb, bio and headshot, and keywords. Keywords help readers find your book, so choose wisely!

5. Upload your Manuscript and Cover Files: You'll also choose your book's trim size, paper color, and whether you want a glossy or matte cover finish.

6. Pricing and Rights: Set your book's price, considering Amazon's printing costs.

7. Order a Proof: Amazon lets you order a physical proof at cost.

8. Publish: Once you're happy, publish your book. It usually takes 24-72 hours for your book to appear on Amazon.

Barnes & Noble Press

Barnes and Noble now has its own print- on demand service, Barnes and Nobel Press. While you can use Ingram Spark to distribute your books to Barnes & Noble, I suggest uploading directly. Yes, it is yet another place you have to upload and manage your book. But the royalties that they pay on their own print-on-demand books are currently 55% versus 40% from other distributors. That can add up quickly for profit for you. They offer lots of different options, including hardcover with a dust jacket.

If your print books are published directly with Barnes & Noble Press, it is easier to get them into their brick-and-mortar stores as an independent author than if you use Ingram Spark.

On the marketing side, if you publish both print and e-books directly with Barnes & Noble, you can be included in their marketing newsletter. This is a service where they promote books that are published within their own ecosystem. It's a nice perk.

Uploading Your Print Book to Barnes & Noble Press

1: Log into your Barnes & Noble Press Account: At press.barnesandnoble.com.

2: Start a New Project: Click on "Create a Print Book" and then select "Start Your Print Book".

3: Enter Book Details: Fill in the book details including the book description, category and subcategory that best fits your book.

4: Upload Manuscript and Cover

6: Choose Book Specifications: Select the book size, binding type, and paper type.

7: **Review and Approve**

8: **Set Pricing:** Barnes & Noble Press will provide a suggested price based on the printing costs.

9. **Set Distribution:** Decide if you want your book to be available only on Barnes & Noble or through other channels as well.

10. **Submit for Review:** Barnes & Noble Press will review your book to ensure it meets their guidelines. This process can take a few days. After your book is approved, you will receive a notification that your book is available for purchase.

Lulu

Founded in 2002, Lulu is the oldest print-on-demand service.

- **Versatility:** Lulu offers a wide range of printing options in terms of book size, paper type, and binding.
- **Distribution:** It has extensive distribution channels, including Amazon, Barnes & Noble, and Lulu's own bookstore.
- **Author-Friendly:** Provides high royalties and control over book pricing.
- **Global Reach:** Has several printing plants outside of the U.S. for international customers.

Steps to Publish with Lulu

1. Create an Account: Sign up on Lulu's website at lulu.com.

2. Choose Your Book's Specifications: Select size, paper, binding, and color options.

3. Upload Your Files: Submit your manuscript, cover, bio, and headshot.

4. Set Your Price

5. Distribution: Choose whether to opt into Lulu's global distribution network. Lulu will distribute your book to various outlets so that you don't have to upload your book multiple times to multiple places. Lulu will print and ship books as orders are placed.

Book Vault

- **Specialized Service:** Book Vault is known for its high-quality printing and a focus on individualized customer service.

- **Wide Product Range:** Offers a variety of print options, including hardcover and color printing.

- **Prints in the U.S. and the U.K**: Book Vault is a British company, but has a printing plant in the U.S.

Steps to Publish with Book Vault

1. Get a Quote: On the Book Vault website at bookvault.app

2. Decide on Specifications: Choose the format, size, paper, and other specifics.

3. Upload Your Manuscript: Provide your formatted manuscript, including your bio and headshot.

4. Upload Your Cover

5. Proofing and Approval: Review a proof of your book before final printing.

6. Order Fulfillment: Book Vault will print and ship books as orders are placed.

What is Bookshop.org?

Bookshop.org is an online bookstore that supports local, independent bookstores, selling only print books. It's an innovative platform that aims to offer a socially conscious alternative to large online retailers. It supports independent bookstores by providing them with a share of the profits from book sales made through the site. For authors, it offers an opportunity to reach readers who prefer supporting local bookstores.

How to Get Your Book on Bookshop.org

1. Bookshop.org does not directly handle the uploading of books. Instead, books are sourced through Ingram Spark.

2. Before your book can appear on Bookshop.org, it needs to be published and available through Ingram Spark.

3. Royalties with Bookshop.org's:

- Bookshop.org earns a commission on books sold, but the exact amount can vary.

- The rest of the profit is split between the author/publisher and the participating independent bookstores.

- Typically, you can expect to earn the standard industry royalty percentages based on the list price of your book.

Take Aways

1. All authors need to have their books on Ingram Spark at , so brick-and-mortar stores and libraries can order copies.

2. Use other print-on-demand services along with Amazon and Barnes & Noble to maximize your reach.

3. Always order a proof copy so you can see what your book looks like before you publish.

4. Consider printing costs and retailer cuts when pricing your books.

Action Steps

1. Upload your book to Ingram Spark.

2. When uploading your book to Ingram Spark, make sure to set your book's distribution settings to include Bookshop.org.

3. Upload your print book files to Amazon.

4. Upload your print book files to Barnes & Noble Press.

5. Decide what other print-on-demand services to use.

Conclusion

Congratulations! You've written and published your first book. You are officially an author! Kudos for having the courage to learn new writing craft and try new things. This journey has shown your dedication, passion, and resilience. Remember, every story you tell is a gift to the world, and your voice matters. Keep creating; keep writing; and keep promoting your books! The world of stories is vast, and your next masterpiece is just waiting to be written. Embrace the journey, and never stop sharing your unique creativity with the world!

Checklists & Resources

Checklist

E-Book and Print Stores

Amazon

- E-books: Decide if you want to be exclusive with Kindle Unlimited.

- Print: If you use KDP Print, your books will be available more quickly than if you use Ingram Spark or Lulu to sell print books on Amazon.

Barnes & Noble

- Print: If you use Barnes & Noble Press, it will be easier to get your book into their brick-and-mortar stores and you will be eligible to be in their newsletter.

Draft2Digital (D2D)

- E-books: Use D2D to distribute your books to the library apps

- E-books: Decide if you want to use D2D to distribute your books to all or some online bookstores.

- Print: Decide if you want to use D2D to upload and distribute your print books to Ingram Spark and other online stores.

E-Books

Kobo

- Opt into their subscription service Kobo Plus because it is not exclusive.

- Choose to be available in all countries.

Apple Books

Google Books

Print

- Ingram Spark
- Bookshop.org

Libraries

- Draft2Digital
- Ingram Spark

Your Local Bookstore

- Ingram Spark

Print on Demand

- To sell on your own website
- For in-person events
- Ingram Spark
- Lulu
- Book Vault

Author Resources

Marketing: Newsletters

- ConvertKit: thepitchmaster.com/convertkit*
- Mailerlite: mailerlite.com/
- ConvertKit's Creator Network and Sparkloop (sparkloop.app) for newsletter referrals to build your list.
- Book Funnel (bookfunnel.com) or Story Origin (storyoriginapp.com) for newsletter swaps.

Website

- AuthorMedia.com a free course - How to Make Your Author Website Amazing - that walks you through building your WordPress site with Divi in a day.

- Divi - WordPress theme - thepitchmaster.com/divi*

- SiteGround - Website hosting - thepitchmaster.com/siteground*

Writing & Publishing

- Scrivener: thepitchmaster.com/scrivener*

- ProWritingAid: thepitchmaster.com/prowritingaid*

- Book Funnel (bookfunnel.com) or Story Origin (storyoriginapp.com) to deliver your reader magnet and digital books and newsletter swaps.

- ISBNs

- U.S.: Bowker - MyIdentifiers.com

- Everywhere else: isbn-international.org

Publishing: Editors

- Reedsy.com
- Editorial Freelancers Association (the-efa.org)

Publishing: Formatting

- Reedsy: (free) reedsy.com/write-a-book
- Draft to Digital: (free) thepitchmaster.com/draft2digital*
- Vellum: (Mac only) vellum.pub
- Attitus: atticus.io/

Publishing: Print on Demand

- Book Vault: bookvault.app
- Lulu : lulu.com/
- Ingram Spark: ingramspark.com/

Publishing: Book Covers

- Reedsy.com

- 100covers.com

Publishing: Stores

- Amazon: kdp.amazon.com
- Barnes and Noble: - press.barnesandnoble.com
- Kobo: kobo.com/us/en/p/writinglife
- Apple Books: itunesconnect.apple.com
- Google Books: play.google.com/books/publish
- Draft to Digital: thepitchmaster.com/draft2digital* (for libraries or everything)

Marketing

- BookBub (bookbub.com/partners) and Written Word Media (writtenwordmedia.com) send emails to readers every day recommending books. Authors can pay to have their books featured.
- Book Brush (bookbrush.com) and Mock Up Shots (mockupshots.com) helps turn your book covers into cool social media images.

- Facebook and Amazon ads

- ChatGPT & Claude for writing blurbs, marketing copy, and marketing.

- Amazon Book Description Generator: kindlepreneur.com/amazon-book-description-generator/

- Publisher Rocket for keywords: publisherrocket.com

- Canva.com for graphic design

Learn

- Joanna Penn's podcast *The Creative Penn* covers all aspects of self-publishing – writing craft, marketing, AI. She has courses and books. www.thecreativepenn.com

- https://kindlepreneur.com/ - free and paid courses, free and paid tools for indie authors. thecreativepenn.com

- Mark Dawson has two courses, Ads for Authors and the Author Launchpad, a podcast, and an annual conference, the Self-Publishing Show Live in London. selfpublishingformula.com

- Author Nation is the biggest indie publishing conference in the world, annually in Las Vegas. (It used to be called 20 Books to 50K) https://www.authornation.live/

- Alliance of Independent Authors is a group that advocates for self-published authors. They also have a podcast, *AskAlli*. allianceindependentauthors.org

- *Wish I'd Known Then* podcast with two indie authors interviewing indie authors about craft and marketing. wishidknownforwriters.com

- *The Novel Marketing Podcast*: authormedia.com/novel-marketing

- *The Author Wheel* Podcast: Two authors interviewing authors about craft and marketing. authorwheel.com

- *The Indy Author Podcast*: indyauthor.com

- Nick Stephenson has courses on how to grow your author career, market, and sell more books. yourfirst10kreaders.com

**These are affiliate links, which means I get a small commission at no extra cost to you. I only recommend things I use in my business.

Publishing Budget

Step 4 Build your email list - Substack - Always free

Step 4 Build your email list - ConvertKit - Free to start

Step 4 Build your email list -MailerLite - Free to start

Step 4 Build your email list – Book Funnel – $20 a year

Step 4 Build your email list – Story Origin – $100 a year

Step 5 Website – SiteGround – web hosting – Watch for sales – $215.88 a year

Step 5 Website – Divi – WordPress theme – $89 a year – $249 purchase

Step 7 Convert Your SP into Prose - Scrivener - $59.99 purchase

Step 11 Hire an Editor..-..ProWritingAid - $120 a year - $144 a year

Step 11 Hire an Editor – Editor – Friend feedback – Prices vary widely

Step 12 Cover – 100covers.com – $100 – $200 – $400

Step 12 Cover – Cover designer – $500 – $1000

Step 17 Formatting – Reedsy.com – free

Step 17 Formatting – Draft2Digital – free

Step 17 Formatting – Atticus – $147 purchase

Step 17 Formatting – Vellum – $249

Step 18 ISBN – ISBN – 1 $125 – 10 $295 – 100 $575

Step 19 Copyright – Copyright – $65

Take Aways & Action Steps

Step 1: Read in Your Genre

Take Aways

1. Reading in your genre will help you improve your prose.

2. You can learn a lot about writing craft and book covers by reading in your genre.

3. Get specific about your subgenre.

4. Genres help in writing, marketing, and selling your book.

Action Steps

1. Check Amazon for the current bestsellers in your genre.

2. Read as many as you can.

Step 2: Read Your Screenplay

Take Aways

1. Read your screenplay to get refamiliarized with your story.

Action Steps

1. Read your screenplay, noticing what you like and don't like about it.

2. Make notes about things you would like to change and add.

Step 3: Write a Scene Breakdown

Take Aways

1. Writing a scene breakdown helps you ana-

lyze your script.

2. Focus on what to cut and add.

3. In a novel you can expand:

4. Subplots

5. Backstories

6. Character arcs

Action Steps

1. Write a scene breakdown, including the logline, characters, purpose, and emotional impact.

2. If you decide to cut scenes, cut them out of both the screenplay and scene breakdown.

3. If you decide to add scenes, add them to the screenplay and scene breakdown with a slugline and logline. This keeps both documents current and will be helpful when you convert the screenplay into novel format.

Step 4: Build Your Email List

Take Aways

1. Email newsletters are a critical part of marketing your book, growing your fan base, and staying in touch with readers.

2. You will need an email marketing service like ConvertKit, MailerLite, or Substack to send your newsletters.

3. A reader magnet is a bonus short story or novella connected to your story world that you use to promote your book and collect emails to grow your list.

4. You can use Story Origin or BookFunnel to send your reader magnet to readers and grow your mailing list with newsletter swaps.

Action Steps

1. Write your reader magnet.

2. Choose an email marketing service. I recommend ConvertKit and MailerLite.

3. Sign up for BookFunnel or Story Origin to deliver your reader magnet and participate in newsletter swaps to grow your list.

4. Add your friends and family to your email list.

5. Start promoting your reader magnet to get subscribers.

Step 5: Build Your Website

Take Aways

1. You need a website to promote your books, screenplays, and creative projects.

2. You can build your website yourself using WordPress.

Action Steps

1. Buy a domain.

2. Sign up for web hosting on a service like SiteGround for WordPress sites.

3. Install WordPress on your site.

4. Pick and install your theme. (I recommend

Divi.)

5. Watch Authormedia.com's course "How to Make Your Author Website Amazing" and build your site.

6. Add your contact information.

7. Add an email subscriber form to your website to grow your email list.

8. To sell your books directly on your website add buy button links to all the online retailers.

Step 6: Choose Your POV

Take Aways

1. The internal monologue is how the reader experiences the main character's thoughts and emotions.

2. The style and voice of the inner monologue should reflect the character's personality, background, and mood.

3. The three most common points of view are: first person (I), third person omniscient (he/she), and limited third (he/she).

4. You can have more than one POV character by alternating chapters.

5. When alternating POV, it is good practice to put the character's name in the chapter title.

Action Steps

1. Try writing the same scene in the three points of view: first person, third person omniscient, and limited third.

2. Choose which POV to use.

3. Consider using alternating POVs.

Step 7: Converting Your Screenplay into Prose with Scrivener

Take Aways

1. Scrivener is designed for writing long documents like novels.

2. The Binder structure makes it easy to drag and drop large pieces of prose.

3. You can keep your research, including your screenplay, in the research folder.

4. You can track your progress with colors and labels.

Action Steps

1. Import your screenplay into Scrivener.

Step 8: Start with the Dialogue

Take Aways

1. Dialogue tags tell the reader who is speaking.

2. Variations of dialogue tags:

- No tags

- He said (I said for first person POV.)

- Character name said

- Using active verbs instead of said

- Using at the end of sentences

- Using in the middle of a sentence

- Adding body language to dialogue and tags

1. Dialogue is interwoven with internal mono-

logue.

2. Dive into your characters' thoughts, feelings, and internal conflicts to enrich the story.

3. Body language is an important part of dialogue.

Action Steps

1. Add dialogue tags to your first scene using the variations discussed.

2. Spend some time on this scene, rewriting using different kinds of tags in different ways until you get a feel for what is going to work for your story.

3. Add dialogue tags to your lines of dialogue using said and other verbs.

4. Use character names and pronouns.

5. Experiment with when and how often you use tags.

6. Add body language.

7. Add your POV character's internal monologue.

- What are they thinking about?
- What are they worried about?
- What do they think about what the other characters are saying?
- Do they believe them?

Step 9: Add Detail

Take Aways

Use prose to:

1. Set the scene.
2. Weave descriptions organically into action or dialogue.
3. Use all five senses in description.
4. Make action sequences detailed.
5. Explore characters' internal thoughts and feelings.
6. Expand on dialogue with internal monologue or narration.
7. Reveal backstory.

8. Add flashbacks and memories.

9. Add subplots.

10. Develop a distinctive narrative voice and style.

Subplots should:

1. Offer different perspectives on the central conflict.

2. Enhance our understanding of the main characters.

3. Introduce tension or complications.

4. Expand on the world or setting.

5. Don't pull focus from the main storyline.

Action Steps

Use the Senses:

1. Go through your scene and add in all the senses.

2. Explore the sensory experiences of your POV character.

3. What emotions and memories do they evoke?

4. Describe the surroundings in your scene.

5. What are the dominant colors, and what's the quality of light?

6. Are there any significant landmarks or unique details that can anchor the scene?

7. Does the setting bring up any emotions or memories?

8. Beyond the spoken words in your scene, what are the background sounds?

9. How does a character react to a sound?

10. What does a character touch?

11. What emotion does it invoke?

12. What are the smells in your scene?

13. How do they make the character feel?

14. Do they evoke any memories?

Add prose to an action sequence:

1. Add some introspection for your POV character.

2. What are they thinking and feeling? Add their emotional reactions.

3. Elongate a moment by adding introspection, setting, and sensory details.

4. Add emotion. What is at stake here for your POV character?

5. Add setting and sensory details.

Write your characters' backstories that are part of your plot.

1. When should you reveal what?

2. Make a note of backstory tidbits in the notes section of the scenes, so you remember to include them.

What are your subplots?

1. How do they connect to the main story?

2. In the notes section of the scenes, put subplot reminders so you can track them.

Step 10: Building Your Novel With Chapters

Take Aways

Each chapter contributes to the narrative progression by:

- Advancing the plot
- Deepening character development
- Enriching the world

A chapter centers on:

- An event
- Conflict
- Theme

A new chapter signals a shift in:

- Time
- Setting
- Mood
- POV

Chapter titles help ground the reader with:

- POV characters
- Place
- Time

Action Steps

1. Make Folders in your Binder. These will be your chapters.

2. Name your chapter folders. These can be placeholder names, so you don't get stuck on this step. Do not name them by numbers because you may move them later.

3. Drag your scenes into their new chapters.

Step 11: Hire an Editor

Take Aways

1. Using an editor helps ensure your book is high quality.

2. There are four types of editors: developmental/book & writing coach, line editor, copy editor, proofreader.

3. The most important for beginning novelists is a developmental editor.

4. Use proofreading software like ProWritingAid.

Action Steps

1. Find three developmental editors/book coaches you are interested in working with.

2. Email them to find out their rates and preferred genres.

3. Ask them for a sample edit of your reader magnet.

4. Hire your editor, making sure that you have in writing the agreed on payment, the scope of the work, and the due date.

Step 12: Design a Cover

Take Aways

1. Your cover and your blurb (Step 13) are the two most important pieces of marketing material to sell your book.

2. Think of your cover as your book's movie poster.

3. Your cover must work as a thumbnail.

4. Covers are genre specific.

5. No DIY. Hire a professional.

6. Use a creative brief to hire your cover designer.

Action Steps

1. Pull or generate reference pictures.

2. Write your creative brief.

Step 13: Write Your Book Blurb

Take Aways

- A book blurb is a brief and engaging description of a book found on the back cover or online product page. It is not a detailed synopsis.

- It's a marketing tool that, together with your cover, helps the reader decide to buy your book.

- A **tagline** is a brief, catchy statement that encapsulates the essence of your book. Use it for the first sentence of your blurb.

- Use generative AI to help you write your blurb if you're stuck.

- Make sure your prompts are specific.
- Always include your genre and best-seller/ing.

The Blurb (Cocktail Pitch) Formula

1. The Emotional Hook
2. Main character and their emotional drive
3. Story Appetizer
4. Cliffhanger

Action Steps

1. Write your blurb.
2. Write your tagline.
3. Practice using AI for blurbs and taglines.

Step 14: Write Your Bio

Take Aways

Bio Formula

1. Your author logline: I write + your genre + kind of books + your personality.

2. Your origin story: It all started with _____ and that's when I realized _____ and now I _____.

3. A personal touch

4. Your favorite things

5. End with a call to action to sign up for your newsletter.

Action Steps

1. Write your bio

Step 15: Get a Headshot

Take Aways

1. A headshot lets your readers see the real you.

2. A headshot is an important compliment to your bio.

Action Steps

1. Take some pictures.

2. Pick your favorite to use as your headshot

with your bio.

Step 16: Write Your Back Matter

Take Aways

1. Back matter is the material in the back of the book after the story.

2. Back matter is prime real estate to sell your next book, give away your lead magnet, get sign ups to your newsletter, and ask for Amazon reviews.

Action Steps

1. Write your call to action to get newsletter subscribers.

2. Write your acknowledgments.

3. Write your author's note.

4. Write your book club discussion questions. (Hint: You can ask Claude or ChatGPT to suggest questions.)

Step 17: Format Your Book

Take Aways

1. Book formatting is designing the interior layout of your book, how the print looks on the page.

2. Book formatting includes choices of font, margins, and chapter design.

3. It is genre specific.

4. There are paid and free software options to format your book.

Action Steps

1. Experiment with the different tools to decide which one you want to use.

2. Don't rush this step. Spend time trying different things to decide what you like.

3. Proofread carefully each formatted copy to make sure there were no software hiccups

Step 18: Get an ISBN

Take Aways

1. You need an ISBN to get copyright and sell books.

2. An ISBN is like your book's Social Security number.

3. You need an ISBN for each format of your book (hardback, paperback, e-book, audio) so, you may consider buying in bulk.

Action Steps

1. Decide how many formats you are publishing.

2. Go to MyIdentifiers.com and set up an account.

3. Purchase your ISBNs.

Step 19: Get Your Copyright

Take Aways

1. An author needs a copyright to protect their original work from being copied or used without their permission.

2. Copyright lasts for the life of the author plus 70 years after her death (in the United States.)

3. Apply online with the Copyright Office to get your copyright.

4. To get your copyright you will need:

- A Manuscript to Upload
- An ISBN
- A credit card for the $65 payment

Action Steps

1. Get your copyright online.

Step 20: Upload Your E-Book to Retailers

Take Aways

1. There are more places to sell your book besides Amazon.

2. Kindle Unlimited is Amazon's subscription. If your book is in KU, you cannot sell e-books anyplace else.

3. Kobo Plus is Kobo's non-exclusive subscription.

4. When pricing your book, remember to include the retailer's cut.

5. Keywords are how readers find your book.

Action Steps

1. Upload your book and cover and keywords to:

- Amazon,

- Barnes and Noble

- Kobo

- Apple Books
- Google Books
- Draft 2 Digital

Step 21: Upload Your Book To Print on Demand Services

Take Aways

1. Print on Demand is a publishing model where books are printed as they are ordered and shipped, rather than in bulk.

2. You can use print on demand to sell physical books:

- On online retailers like Amazon, Barnes & Noble, and Bookshop.org.
- At brick-and-mortar stores like your local bookshop.
- On your own website.
- To libraries.
- At live events like conventions, conferences, and book signings.

1. Ingram Spark is the catalog that bookstores and libraries order from.
2. Amazon and Barnes & Noble have their own print on demand services.
3. Order a proof copy to check how your book looks.

Action Steps

1. Upload your book to:

- Ingram Spark
- Amazon
- Barnes & Noble

1. Order Proofs
2. Choose a POD service for your website.

- Lulu
- Book Vault

2. Order a proof.
3. Order author copies

Acknowledgements

Thank you to my parents for their unwavering support of this book and all my creative endeavors. I am so lucky that my parents are my biggest fans. Thank you, Penny, Lynn, and Olive!

Thank you to Mike Tabb, who graciously let me use his script, *The Casanovas*, to practice importing and formatting in Scrivener. This is one of my favorite scripts and I hope to read it as a novel someday soon.

Thank you to Keith Houk for reading the book and giving me valuable feedback.

Thank you to Thomas Umstattd Jr. and the Novel Marketing Conference for igniting my excitement for marketing. Thank you to Jeff Elkins for teaching me how to write amazing dialogue.

Thank you to John Gaspard, whose novel *The Sword and Mr. Stone* inspired me to write this book. As I was reading his novel, I kept thinking this reads like a movie. Then, I heard him on a podcast talking about how the project started off as a script.

Thank you to my editor, Jalinna Jones whose eagle eyes helped me level up my book.

Thank you to all the writers out there whose scripts I have read over the years. Your stories excite and thrill me. I can't wait to read your books.

And finally, thank you to all my clients whose stories, enthusiasm, and dedication inspire me every day.

Keep writing and creating!

About the Author

Lindsey loves helping people discover their superpower, create compelling content, and become excited about pitching and networking. She teaches how to pitch like a boss, network like a VIP, and write like an Oscar winner.

In her wide-ranging career as a Hollywood development executive, Lindsey has worked on everything from feature films, television movies and TV series, to animation and live action. She began her career reading scripts for Robert Zemeckis and Kathryn Bigelow; worked under Michael Eisner at Walt Disney Feature Animation; and developed projects for John H. Williams, producer of the billion dollar *Shrek* franchise.

She is the author of two books, *How to Turn Your Screenplay Into a Novel* and *The Pitch Master's Top Tactics*. For help with storytelling and networking, she may be reached at thepitchmaster.com. Subscribe to her weekly newsletter for actionable creativity and career tips at thepitchmaster.com/newsletter.

If you enjoyed this book, please leave a review on Amazon, Good Reads, or your favorite bookstore.

Also by

The Pitch Master's Top Tactics

Milton Keynes UK
Ingram Content Group UK Ltd.
UKHW020810210824
447217UK00007B/54